T0322203

Praise for *The Happiness Cure*

'Kidneys evolve. Lungs evolve. As do brains, and in ways relevant to our pursuit of happiness and our vulnerabilities to mental illness. In *The Happiness Cure*, psychiatrist Anders Hansen explains how our brains have evolved more slowly in these realms than has our life-style, and the malaise that this mismatch produces. This wonderful book is steeped in insights, clear explanations and empathy. Most of all, it imparts deep wisdom about how we should live our lives.'

Robert Sapolsky, Professor of Biology and Neurology at Stanford University, and *New York Times* bestselling author

'A brilliantly researched book that will transform how you think about happiness.'

Thomas Erikson, international bestselling author of *Surrounded by Idiots*

'Anders Hansen's work is the antidote to our modern-day struggles.'

Dr Rangan Chatterjee, bestselling author and creator of the podcast *Feel Better, Live More*

'A fascinating exploration of the ways in which our ancient neuro-logic wiring is mismatched for the modern ecosystem. By understanding depression and anxiety through the lens of evolution, we can make sense of the growing despair in the world today and do something about it. This is a must-read for anyone hoping to under-stand the human brain.'

Dr Anna Lembke, Professor at Stanford University, *New York Times* bestselling author of *Dopamine Nation*

the
mind-body
method

OTHER BOOKS BY ANDERS HANSEN

The Happiness Cure (2023)

The Attention Fix (2023)

The ADHD Advantage (2024)

the mind-body method

How Moving Your Body Can Stop You Losing Your Mind

Dr Anders Hansen

Vermilion
LONDON

1

Vermilion, an imprint of Ebury Publishing
20 Vauxhall Bridge Road
London SW1V 2SA

Vermilion is part of the Penguin Random House group of companies
whose addresses can be found at global.penguinrandomhouse.com

First published by Bonnier Fakta in 2016

This edition published by Vermilion in 2024

www.penguin.co.uk

A CIP catalogue record for this book is available from the British Library

ISBN 9781785044366

Typeset in 10.5/15.5pt ITC Galliard Pro by Jouve (UK), Milton Keynes.
Printed and bound in Great Britain by Clays Ltd, Elcograf S.p.A.

The authorised representative in the EEA is Penguin Random House Ireland,
Morrison Chambers, 32 Nassau Street, Dublin D02 YH68

Penguin Random House is committed to a sustainable future
for our business, our readers and our planet. This book is made
from Forest Stewardship Council® certified paper.

CONTENTS

FOREWORD

WHAT IS THE best exercise for the brain? Had I been asked that question 15 years ago, I would probably have guessed crossword puzzles or Sudokus. But to the surprise of many, the answer is physical exercise! Physical exercise not only makes us feel better, it also improves all our cognitive functions. It boosts our memory, sharpens our attention and makes us more creative. It even seems to affect our intelligence – in the right direction, I should add!

This may seem strange but it is backed up by decades of neuroscientific research. We have seen an explosion of studies that confirm the effects of exercise on our cognition. But what I have found most striking as a psychiatrist is the effect of exercise on mood and well-being. Exercise not only reduces our risk of anxiety and depression, but can also be used to treat these conditions as effectively as antidepressants or therapy. I have taken this knowledge to heart and often prescribe exercise to my patients. Of course, I still prescribe medication and therapy as well, but I view exercise to be as important as treatment – and that is a viewpoint supported by science.

Personally, I have always been physically active. I loved playing soccer when I was growing up and I have continued to exercise during my adult life. But when I read all the studies and learned how exercise strengthens the brain, I started taking it more seriously and made sure never to miss it – not because I wanted to become good at a particular sport, but because I knew my brain needed it. Then it slowly dawned on me that if I felt motivated from learning this, maybe others might as well. That is how the idea for the book you are holding came to me.

I worked on *The Mind-Body Method* for almost two years. I wanted it to be packed with science and facts, but I also wanted it to be exciting to read. I wrote, rewrote and rewrote it again to make sure the knowledge was accessible. My goal was that everyone would understand it, not just those who are interested in psychology and neuroscience. I wanted to show the mechanisms through which exercise boosts the brain and how much exercise you need to do to reap these benefits. Beyond that, I wanted my readers to ponder exercise in an evolutionary light and not only learn *how* it affects the brain but *why* it does so. Humans are built for movement, but fear not – exercise has nothing to do with being good at a sport. It is about riding a bike to work instead of taking the car. It is about doing some gardening or taking a walk instead of watching TV. Anything that involves movement works, and the brain counts every step – not how, where or when we take them.

I hoped that *The Mind-Body Method* would be an interesting read for a couple of thousand people. I did not dream that the book would sell more than 700,000 copies in my native Sweden; it is staggering to think that 7 per cent of my country's population has bought it. But the greatest pay-off is not sales figures or chart positions, it is the feedback from people who – through emails, letters and on the street – have told me how this book motivated them to become more physically active. More or less all of them say the book provided the spark for a change in their lifestyle that has made them both feel and function better. Even though I always tell them that they should not thank me, they should thank themselves since they have done all the work, I must admit it makes me proud. I know their new lifestyle means they have improved their chances of living a longer and healthier life. To play a small part in that, in a way to be a doctor to someone you have not met, is . . . well, it's just awesome!

Since *The Mind-Body Method* was first published, many more scientific studies have been published that confirm what I wrote in the book. I am happy that it is still so relevant and, had I written it today, I would have written exactly the same book.

In fact, this book is even more relevant today. The Covid-19 pandemic made us more sedentary and more glued to our screens than ever, and that has cost human lives. Major studies have shown that exercise reduces your risk of being hospitalised and needing intensive care for Covid-19 by about 50 per cent. Let me repeat that: exercise cuts your risk of getting severely sick in half. It does not make you immune to the virus, but it does make you less likely to become severely sick and die if you catch it. And Covid-19 is just one of many diseases. Exercise also reduces the risk of diabetes, cardiovascular disease, breast cancer and colon cancer. However, although these protective effects are eyebrow raising, they are seldom motivating. Very few people will change their habits from knowing that the risk of a future disease is knocked down by a number of percentage points. Humans have not evolved to think about what will happen to them in the future; we have evolved for the here and now! That is why the effects of exercise on the brain are so important – they *are* here and now! You will be more focused *now* if you move. You will be more creative *now*. You will be more tolerant to stress *now*.

I hope that you find *The Mind-Body Method* interesting. Even more, I hope you find it motivating and that it gives you a small push towards a longer, healthier, happier and more productive life!

Anders Hansen
January 2024

PREFACE: EXERCISE YOUR BRAIN

MAKE TWO FISTS and join them together side by side. This is the size of your brain. It weighs about the same as a carton of milk. Imagine something this small containing everything you have ever felt and experienced. All your personality traits. Everything you have ever learned. All your memories – from your first, faint mental images of a summer vacation when you were three, through your childhood and teenage years, to your current, grown-up life where you are now reading these words.

Everything is stored in that lump, the most complex structure we know of in the universe, which consumes no more energy than a light bulb. Whoever isn't fascinated by the brain can't be intrigued by much.

While we've known for some time how the body's other organs work, the brain has remained a mystery – until now. Thanks to recently developed research tools, our knowledge has made great leaps in the past decades. We have begun to understand, in detail, how the brain functions. Today, few question not only that we have a brain but that we *are* our brain.

Brain research has given us a biological glimpse at human characteristics, but the biology of your brain doesn't set in stone what sort of person you will be. Studies have brought to light just how fantastically malleable the brain can be in both children and adults. New brain cells are developing constantly. Connections are created and disappear. Everything you do, every thought you have, modifies the brain a little bit. Your brain is more akin to modelling clay than china.

So how do you shape this clay? Well, there are few things as important for your brain as moving your body. Not only do you feel better when you're physically active, your concentration, memory, creativity and resistance to stress are also improved. You're able to process information more quickly – you actually *think* faster – and you become more adept at mobilising your intellectual resources as needed. You gain access to an extra 'mental gear' to help you focus when things get hectic around you, and to stay calm when your thoughts start racing. In fact, physical activity even seems to increase your level of intelligence.

Doesn't that sound strange? After all, if we want stronger arms, we train our arms, not our legs. The same should apply to the brain: if we want a brain that functions better, surely we ought to train it with crosswords, memory exercises and other brain gymnastics? As it turns out, that's not true. Research clearly indicates that memory exercises, Sudokus and crosswords don't come close to boosting the brain as positively as engaging in regular physical activity. Surprisingly, the brain seems to be the organ that benefits the most from our being in motion.

In this book, I'm going to show you the huge impact that exercise and training have on your brain, and explain the reasons why. Some of the results are noticeable immediately – as in, right after you've been for a walk or a run – while others require regular training for at least a year in order to take effect. I will also describe

THE MIND-BODY METHOD

specifically what you need to do to achieve the outcomes and mental advantages that research has shown physical activity provides – benefits that amount to no less than a mental upgrade.

Enjoy!

Chapter 1

YOUR CHANGEABLE BRAIN

The chief function of the body is to carry the brain around.
THOMAS A. EDISON

IMAGINE YOU'RE SITTING in a time machine and you've cranked the year back to 10,000 BC. The machine starts clanging and suddenly you're hurled thousands of years back in time. You nervously step out of the capsule and look around. A group of people dressed in animal hides are standing there and they seem surprised to see you.

What is your first impression of them? That they're primitive cave dwellers who might, at best, be able to hunt down an animal and kill it, but who are otherwise incapable of showing any hint of advanced thought? One is tempted to think that, but as it happens you and they are very much alike. Of course, they don't speak the same language as you and they have a completely different set of experiences, but overall they function quite similarly to you. They possess the same cognitive abilities and the same feelings you do. We humans have not changed all that much, really, over the past 12,000 years.

By contrast, our lifestyle has undergone immense transformation in just 100 years, and if you look back as far as 12,000 years, the degree of change is unbelievable. You live in material comfort and make use of technical tools the likes of which your ancient predecessors could not have conceived in their wildest dreams. You exist in entirely different social environments. You probably meet as many fresh faces in a single week as they would over the course of their entire lives.

There is another fundamental difference between your way of life and that of those who came before you: they moved considerably more than you do. Taken in historical context, they are not alone in this. Over hundreds of thousands of years our ancestors were significantly more physically active than we are today, and the reason is simple: throughout most of human history it was necessary to be physically active in order to procure food and survive. Consequently, not only are our bodies built for movement, so are our brains.

12,000 years seems like an eternity but from a biological perspective, it is a short period. Evolution often requires considerably more time than that for big changes to occur in a species, and this applies to us humans and our brain, too. Despite the enormous changes we have made to our lifestyle that have removed us further and further from the life we evolved for, our brain is still adapted to a life on the savanna. This is especially true when it comes to how much we move. Even though we don't need to hunt for our food any more and can now order our groceries online, our brains still run more efficiently when we live a little more like our ancestors did – and when we move our bodies.

EXERCISE AND TRAINING PRODUCE A MORE EFFICIENT BRAIN

I've read thousands of studies over the years, and if I had to pick the one that fascinated me the most, the one that changed not only my view of medicine and health but also to a certain degree my view of life in general, it would be the one in which the brains of about one hundred 60-year-old human test subjects were examined by magnetic resonance imaging (MRI).

MRI is nothing short of a technical miracle for brain researchers; it is a tool that has truly opened us up to another world. Today, thanks to MRI, we can look inside the cranium and get a picture, in real time, of how the brain works while we think and perform different tasks, at no risk of injury to the person being examined.

The goal of this one particular study was to understand the effects of ageing on the brain, because our brain – just like our skin, heart and lungs – does get old. But *how* does it age, really? And are we doomed to go through the ageing process with no means of influencing it, or are we able to alter its course in any way, perhaps by engaging in regular physical activity? This is what researchers began to suspect after animal trials demonstrated that the brains of caged mice who could run on a wheel tended to age more slowly.

For the study's authors to answer these questions, the 60-year-old participants were split into two groups: one in which the subjects took regular walks a few times a week over the course of one year, and one in which the people met as often as the other group but performed easy exercises that did not increase their heart rate.

The test subjects' brains were examined by MRI prior to the study, and again one year after the study. To observe the participants' brain processes, the MRIs took place while the subjects were performing a set of psychological tests. The scans revealed how different parts of the brain were being activated, and how areas in the temporal lobe worked together with areas in the occipital lobe and the frontal lobe in what appeared to be a sophisticated network.

However, the most telling revelation lay not in the results per se, but in the contrast those results showed between the study's two test groups.

The participants who walked didn't just get in better shape over the course of the year, they also developed more effective brains. The MRIs showed that the connections between the lobes had strengthened, most notably the connections between the temporal lobe and both the frontal and occipital lobes. In short, different sections of the brain were better integrated with one another, which meant, quite simply, that the entire organ functioned more efficiently. Somehow the physical activity – i.e. the walks – had had a positive impact on the brain's connectivity pattern.

When the results from the 60-year-olds' MRI scans were compared to the younger participants' scans, the researchers found they looked similar. The brains of the 60-year-olds who had been physically active appeared to have become biologically younger. The most striking effect was the connection between the frontal and the temporal lobe, which is the area of the brain that tends to be most affected by ageing. Seeing improvement in that particular area indicated that the ageing process of the whole brain had stalled.

But more importantly, in addition to yielding measurable results on the scans the regular walks made a real, practical difference. Psychological tests showed that the set of cognitive functions called 'executive control' or 'executive function' – which among other things include the ability to take initiative, to plan and to have attentional control – showed improvement in the group of test subjects who regularly walked.

Simply put, this discovery indicates that the brain works more efficiently in people who are physically active, and that the effects of ageing can be halted or even reversed to make the brain more energetic.

Take a minute to think about what you've just read. Go over it again. If that isn't enough to motivate you to start exercising, I don't know what will. You know that you'll improve your stamina by running and that you'll develop bigger muscles by lifting weights, but you probably weren't aware that exercise and training can also bring about changes in your brain – changes that are not only measurable by modern medical technology but are also extremely important to optimal cognitive function.

We're going to examine these changes in more detail later in this book, but first we're going to look at how the brain works, and then we'll see how it can be made to operate better.

YOUR INNER UNIVERSE

The brain has shown itself to be rather more malleable than we were led to believe until recently. What you have inside your cranium isn't some kind of advanced computer with genetically preprogrammed functions destined to develop in a certain way; the brain is far more complex than that. It contains approximately 86 billion (86,000,000,000) brain cells. Each cell can connect to thousands of other cells, which means that the number of possible connections in the brain totals at least 86 *trillion* (86,000 billion). That is about 500 times more than the number of stars in the Milky Way. To say that you have your own universe inside your skull might sound somewhat New Age-y, but it is actually an accurate metaphor.

> **Every sensation you experience, every thought you have – everything leaves a trace and changes you a little.**

The universe in your head is enormously active. Old brain cells die and new cells are created continuously. Connections are made between the cells and connections are lost if they are not used. The strength of those connections changes over time depending on how the brain redesigns its architecture. You can look at the brain as a highly sophisticated ecosystem in a state of constant flux. These changes keep happening throughout your life, not only when you are a child or when you learn something new. Every sensation you experience, every thought you have – everything leaves a trace and changes you a little. The brain you have today is not quite the same as the one you had yesterday. The brain is a continuous *work in progress.*

It is *not* – as some believe – the number of brain cells or the size of the brain that determines whether a brain functions well. The most telling example is Albert Einstein, whose brain was neither bigger nor heavier than the average human brain. Einstein's brain weighed 1,230g (2.7lb), compared to the 1,350g (3.0lb) of the average man's brain and compared to the average woman's brain, which weighs approximately 100g (3.5oz) less.

For a long time, I believed it was the number of connections between brain cells that determined the brain's capacity, but that's not right either. Two-year-old children have significantly more connections between brain cells than adults do. As a child grows, the number of connections decreases. This process is called 'pruning', and it's estimated that up to 20 billion connections disappear *every 24 hours* from the age of two to adolescence. The brain weeds out unused connections to make room for the ones that carry signals – which can be neatly summarised as: *neurons that fire together, wire together.*

But if neither the number of brain cells nor the number of connections between them determines the quality of a brain, what does? The answer is that when we do different things – swimming, cycling or signing your name, for instance – the brain uses a type of 'program' called a functional network. You have a program for swimming, another for cycling and a third for writing your signature. Everything you do is dependent on these networks, which are all basically built from a collection of brain cells that are connected to one another. A program can integrate cells from many different areas of the brain, and for it to run optimally – to enable you to swim, ride a bike or sign something – it is necessary for the brain's different areas to be closely interconnected.

Practice makes perfect – and more agile – brain programs

Imagine you'd like to learn to play a simple tune on the piano. Many different areas in the brain must work together to make that possible. For a start, you'll need to see the keys. A signal goes from the eyes through the optic nerve to the primary visual cortex in the occipital lobe. Simultaneously, the motor cortex (in the brain) must coordinate the movements of your hands and fingers. The auditory cortex processes sound information and sends it to areas called 'association areas' in the temporal and parietal lobes. The information eventually reaches the frontal lobe, the seat of higher brain functions, and you become aware of what you are playing and can correct any wrong notes you hit. All this activity to play a simple piano tune!

All these areas in the visual and auditory centrums, the motor cortex, the parietal and frontal lobes are part of the brain's program for playing music. The more you practise, the better you become at it, and the more efficiently the program runs in your brain. At the beginning it will take a great deal of effort to play the tune. The program is inefficient and awkward and requires that big chunks of the brain be fully engaged in the task. That's why you'll experience playing the piano as mentally taxing and you will need to focus hard to accomplish the task.

In time, as you continue to practise, it will become easier; once you've put in a tremendous amount of work, you will be able to play the tune while thinking about something else. The brain's program for playing the tune has now become efficient at transferring information; a repeated signal through the network has strengthened the connection: *neurons that fire together, wire together.* In the end, less and less mental effort will be required, and you'll be able to play the tune without giving it a second thought.

As the program for playing the tune activates cells from different areas of the brain, those different areas need to be closely connected for the program to run well. We can compare it to a computer, where all the different components need to be connected in order to work. If the connections are bad, the computer won't run, even if each input works well independently.

The connections reveal how you live your life

It may sound a bit strange that different areas of the brain can be connected to each other to different degrees, but research has shown that this could be an important reason why cognitive abilities vary between people. Fascinating findings have recently been uncovered in this specific area of research.

Advanced brain testing on hundreds of individuals has revealed that different parts of the brain are closely interconnected in people with sets of qualities that are deemed to be 'positive', such as good memory function and concentration, higher education and a cautious, negligible intake of alcohol and tobacco. In subjects with 'negative' qualities, such as poor anger management, smoking and alcohol or drug abuse, the opposite pattern has been observed: these areas of the brain are badly connected to each other.

You can see roughly how a person leads their life by looking at their brain's connectivity pattern.

That many positive qualities leave an identical imprint on the brain, and that negative qualities seem to make the opposite type of mark, implies that there is a 'positive–negative axis' along which we can all be placed depending on how we live. The scientists who performed this study believe that you can see roughly how a person leads their life by looking at their brain's connectivity pattern.

So is there anything else that's considered positive along that positive–negative axis, apart from good memory, higher education and caution around alcohol? Indeed there is: being in good physical shape.

YOUR LIFESTYLE SHAPES YOUR BRAIN

The debate about whether we are shaped by our genes or our environment has ebbed and flowed over a long time, often veering from one extreme point of view to another, more stringent opinion. Today we know it is *neither* our genetic make-up *nor* our environment that decides our fate exclusively, but a combination of both. We also know that genes and environment are closely interwoven: the environment affects our genes – our DNA – through incredibly complex biological mechanisms.

There are a few numbers that clearly illustrate that it isn't only your genetic make-up that decides how your brain will develop and how you will turn out as a human being. You possess approximately 23,000 genes. You also have about 86 billion brain cells, which in turn have around 86,000 billion connections between them. Your 23,000 genes can't possibly hold sway over those 86,000 billion connections. Quite simply, the brain is far too complex to be governed by an exact, predetermined genetic programme that is in charge of the brain's development throughout life.

Your genes set the stage for how your brain cells will be created and die, and how they will connect and disconnect from one another. Exactly how this happens, which characteristics you develop and how you function mentally will be influenced by your life experiences, by the type of environment you live in and, not least, by the lifestyle you adopt.

The aspect of our lifestyle that this book is all about – physical exercise – is, naturally, not the only factor that influences how our brain develops, but research shows that it plays a pivotal role and is far more important than most are aware of.

Judgemental research?

You might believe that this type of research is judgemental or elitist; after all, the mere fact that we are talking about a positive–negative axis suggests a sort of ranking of people. I completely understand how it could be interpreted that way, but I also believe that some people may misconstrue the results of these tests. Our *inherent qualities* are not what primarily affect our brain's connectivity pattern, nor where we happen to be situated along the positive–negative axis. Instead, it is our lifestyle that does this. Through the *choices* we make, we can change our brain's operating mode on a more fundamental level than we previously thought. It isn't just our brain that decides how we think and act; our thoughts and actions can also modify our brain and how it works. We run our brains, not the other way around. From this angle, we can see how the most important thing for improving the connection between different parts of our brain might be to partake in regular physical exercise, and how being in good physical condition produces a positive reading on the positive–negative axis.

THE MIND-BODY METHOD

NEUROPLASTICITY: HOW THE BRAIN CHANGES THROUGHOUT LIFE

I wish I had learned to play an instrument as a kid. Now it's too late.
Many of us have had this thought at one time or another. The fact is,
the brain is extremely malleable during childhood, which makes
learning everything from languages to motor skills swift and natural.
But why is it that a child's brain can learn so much in such a short
time, with little obvious effort?

A youngster must quickly learn to navigate the world. This is
evident in their brain from the cells' enormous ability not only to
create connections with one another but also to break them off (i.e.
pruning). This happens at a rate that will, as you've noticed, never
come back later in life. The brain's capacity for change – which in
scientific parlance is referred to as 'neuroplasticity' – is perhaps its
most important quality, because even if its flexibility is never as great
as when we are children, it doesn't vanish entirely. It's still there –
even in adults, even in 80-year-olds. To see exactly how influenceable
and changeable an adult brain is, we're going to look at what happened to Michelle Mack, a 42-year-old American woman whose
remarkable life story has changed our understanding of what the
human brain is truly capable of.

The woman who only had half her brain

Michelle Mack was born in Virginia in November 1973. As early as
a few weeks after her birth, her parents noticed something was not
right. Michelle was unable to steady her gaze and she didn't move
normally, especially her right arm and leg. Her parents took her to
numerous specialists to examine her eyes and to see if she had cerebral palsy, which she did not. None of the neurologists they consulted
could explain Michelle's symptoms, and neither could an X-ray of her

brain. In the early 1970s, our modern technologies – such as the computerised axial tomography (CAT) scan and MRI – were still in the early stages of development.

At the age of three, Michelle still wasn't walking and she could hardly speak. Her physician recommended that they schedule a new CAT scan, since medical diagnostic techniques had advanced since her first examination.

The result of the scan performed in 1977 shocked Michelle's parents and her physicians. Michelle was missing virtually the entire left side of her brain, probably due to something that had happened to her while she was still an embryo. She was living with only half a brain.

One possible explanation is that Michelle had suffered a stroke before birth; another is that her left carotid artery had been blocked, depriving the left side of her brain of blood. No one could provide a definitive answer, but one thing was crystal clear: more than 90 per cent of the left side of Michelle's brain was missing.

The left side of the brain is commonly thought of as the analytical and rational part, the seat of mathematical and linguistic thinking, while the right side is more artistic and creative. Even though we now realise that this divvying up of the brain is an oversimplification, it isn't too far from reality. Bearing in mind the set of responsibilities held by the left side of the brain, many of Michelle's difficulties suddenly made sense. Her inability to speak properly could be explained by the missing linguistic part of her brain. And since the left side of the brain would also have been in charge of the mobility of the right side of the body (and vice versa), it was no wonder she had trouble moving her right arm and leg.

However, it isn't Michelle's early years that make her so fascinating, but what happened to her later. She successively developed the abilities she had been lacking, and at a rate her physicians had not dared hope for. She learned to walk, speak and read, and she other-wise developed somewhat normally, if a little more slowly than most of her peers.

Today Michelle lives a normal life in many ways and works part time in her parish. Her ability to find words is mostly normal, even though that function is usually found in the part of the brain that she is missing. Although the mobility in her right arm and leg is still limited, she has no problem walking.

Tests have shown that Michelle has some difficulty with abstract thinking, but she has a phenomenal memory for detail. This gives her a highly unusual skill: she can immediately tell you what day of the week corresponds with a randomly selected date. Ask Michelle what day of the week 18 March 2010 fell on and she'll correctly answer 'Thursday' almost instantly.

The right half of Michelle's brain has taken over handling many of the tasks her left brain would normally deal with. We know from past studies that this can be done on a smaller scale, but few scientists had speculated that such a massive restructuring of the brain – one that could compensate for a missing half – was possible. The rewiring of Michelle's brain is so extensive that her brain's right half actually looks a bit crowded. In fact, Michelle has issues with visuospatial orientation, i.e. the ability to judge distance and spatial orientation. Visuospatial orientation is normally found in the right side of the brain (which is intact for Michelle), but it is believed that since her right brain is pulling double duty – handling responsibilities for both the right and the missing left side – there just isn't enough room in there for all its regular functions.

It's probably no accident that Michelle can immediately match a specific date to its corresponding day of the week. The two halves of our brain work as a kind of brake for each other and, as strange as it may sound, inhibit the function of the other half. Why would the brain limit itself? It could be to restrain the other half if it grows too strong within a certain area, so that we achieve balance in our cerebral abilities and acquire reasonable abilities in many areas, instead of becoming extremely adept at some and very poor at others. But if the halves of the brain are unable to communicate, the equilibrium might be lost and then certain abilities can blossom, often to the detriment of others.

The human Google

This is exactly what is believed to have happened to the American Kim Peek, the inspiration for Dustin Hoffman's role as Raymond Babbitt in the movie *Rain Man*. Kim was born with an injury to the corpus callosum, a band of nerve fibres that forms the most important link between the left and right sides of the brain. Kim's injury caused a faulty connection in this link, and so he didn't learn to walk until he was 4 years old. He was considered to be so severely mentally disabled that doctors suggested he be institutionalised.

But just like Michelle, Kim recovered and developed in ways no one could have foreseen. At around five years old he learned to read, and whenever he finished a book he placed it front cover down. His parents were astonished at the speed with which the house filled up with down-facing books. By then Kim was also beginning to show a mind-boggling memory for detail, perhaps the best ever documented in a human being. He could read two pages of a book simultaneously, the left side with his left eye and the right side with his right eye. It took him ten seconds to read one page; he could go through an entire book in an hour. His favourite pastime was going to the public library, where he read eight books a day.

Kim remembered everything in the approximately 12,000 books he had read. He kept in his head an unimaginable number of facts of varying degrees of importance about everything from Shakespeare to American zip codes to the British royal family. If anyone deserves to be called the 'human Google', it's Kim Peek.

As with Michelle Mack, Kim could also immediately tell you which weekday a date corresponded to, whether it was several decades in the future or in the past. People often told Kim their date of birth and asked him what day it was. Not only did he immediately give them the correct answer – 'You were born on a Sunday' – but he could also add, 'You will turn 80 on a Friday.'

Kim's abilities were so unique that he has been called 'Kimputer' and 'mega-savant', but his life was far from simple. He was often awkward in social situations and was barely able to dress himself. He also tested quite a bit below average on IQ tests, despite his extraordinary memory. Kim was always generous and volunteered his time whenever neuroscientists asked him to, and his unique case has provided us with important clues about how memory works. It is now believed that Kim's outsized memory was a result of his brain's halves lacking the ability to balance each other out.

THE BRAIN'S PROGRAMS CAN BE REWRITTEN

There are similarities as well as differences between Kim Peek and Michelle Mack. In Michelle's case the connection between the two halves of her brain was not absent – half her brain was simply not there. But the missing half might very well have had the same effect as a bad link between two existing brain halves, ensuring that certain abilities grew uncontrollably and gave rise to exceptional qualities.

Michelle and Kim are perhaps the best examples of neuroplasticity – the brain's superb ability to reorganise itself – and there's no longer any doubt that the brain's structure and operating mode are changeable, not only for Michelle and Kim, but also for you and me.

But why have I devoted so much time to these two people's stories in a book about the effects of exercise and athletic training on the brain? The reason is very simple: it is important to show that the brain *can* change, because not everyone is aware of this. So what creates this change? This is how we end up on the topic of physical activity and working out.

There are few things as effective in making the brain changeable as being physically active.

DO WE ONLY USE 10 PER CENT OF OUR BRAIN?

It's time to put to rest the myth that we only use 10 per cent of our brain. It's not unreasonable to think that you might only be using 10 per cent of your brain while reading this sentence. It's also not impossible that you might only use 10 per cent of your brain when you go for a bike ride, although it's not necessarily the same 10 per cent you press into service when you're reading. In actuality, we work our entire brain – but different parts of it depending on what we're up to.

Today we know that electrical activity and the use of glucose and oxygen – the brain's main fuels – are continuous processes in the brain. This means it is always active; no area is idle in a healthy brain. The brain would never allow 90 per cent of its capacity to stay dormant. Considering our brain's phenomenal ability to move different functions around (just think back to Michelle Mack), it would quickly put any quiet area to good use.

The idea that we only use 10 per cent of our brain is also obviously a myth when we account for energy consumption. The brain devours a substantial amount of energy – about 20 per cent of all the energy required by the body – even though it only makes up 2 per cent of our body's total weight. This means that it uses more than ten times the energy per kilogram than the rest of the body. From an evolutionary standpoint, such an energy-draining organ wouldn't have been permitted to grow if it were unnecessary. The cost of a large brain is that it requires more food, and thus more time is needed to seek out this food. If the brain were indeed 90 per cent inactive, the time and energy expended to find food would be a huge misuse of resources. Such a wastrel would not have survived long on the path of natural selection.

More like modelling clay than china

In the study of neuroplasticity, it has been shown that there are few things as effective in making the brain changeable – that is, neuroplastic – as being physically active. It also appears that the activity does not need to last an especially long time. The fact is, just 20–30 minutes is enough to affect neuroplasticity.

One of the mechanisms that converts your running steps into a changeable brain involves an amino acid called gamma-aminobutyric acid (GABA). GABA acts like a brake on the brain, inhibiting activity and making sure nothing changes. But GABA's influence ebbs when you become physically active, because exercise removes its block against change, thus making the brain more flexible and better at reorganising itself. If we consider the brain from a 'more like modelling clay than china' perspective, the change in GABA activity makes the clay softer and more malleable. Thus the brain of a person who trains becomes more like a child's, and GABA is involved in that process.

Hopefully you have realised by now how changeable the brain is, and that exercise plays a big role in this changeability since it can modify and streamline our brain's programs. Results become apparent in many different areas, and we will now look a bit more closely at those areas, specifically at the impact that training has on our mental functions. We'll start with something that afflicts many people today: stress and anxiety.

CHAPTER 2

RUN AWAY FROM STRESS

Whenever we feel stressed out, it's a sign that our brain is pumping out stress hormones. If sustained over months and years, those hormones can ruin our health and turn us into nervous wrecks.

DANIEL GOLEMAN, AUTHOR AND PSYCHOLOGIST

The stress begins as soon as I open my eyes in the morning. Earlier than that, actually, because it is often stress that wakes me up. It feels like my brain is racing 24/7. I spend the entire day thinking about what I should do, and in the evening the anxiety continues to grind at me without any real reason for it to do so.

I live a hectic life. I do enjoy my job as a business attorney, but I wish it weren't so time consuming. I have a lot going on outside of work, too. I have two small children, so I always have a guilty conscience because I'm not always on time to pick them up from daycare; then there's everything else that needs to be planned. Sometimes it seems as though life is just a round of logistics. But even though I have a lot to do at home and at work, I know I would have time for it all if I didn't stress about it so much. The stress stops me and I often feel blocked.

The stress has increased lately – either that or I'm less able to handle it. I have memory lapses and I have become more and more absentminded. I forgot my laptop in a restaurant after lunch, and it wasn't until I got back to the office that I realised I had left it behind. It was sheer luck that it was still there. This kind of thing never happened before.

The other day I was on the bus, and it was packed; suddenly I found it hard to breathe and had such a feeling of anxiety that I almost panicked. I ended up getting off a few stops early and walking the rest of the way. This has never happened before either.

I MET WITH this 37-year-old man in a psychiatric clinic's outpatient office. He told me how he had been feeling lately. He was a bit apprehensive to begin with and tried to downplay his problems as though he was ashamed, but eventually he became more open. The level of stress he had been experiencing over several years had gotten worse over time. He had trouble sleeping and became irritated over the smallest trifle. He had been hiding his angst carefully from those around him. But what did this man – married, with two children, a good job and a big apartment – have to be unhappy about? All the outward signs of a successful life were there, but still something was not right.

After almost an hour of talking, I explained to him that he seemed to have been under a high amount of pressure over a prolonged stretch of time, and that his symptoms – deteriorating memory, trouble sleeping and the panic attack – most likely had their roots in this. He could consider antidepressant medication, but he did not want that. He asked if there were other options and I explained to him that talking therapy is usually effective, and that he should also begin an exercise programme by taking up running. That sounded odd to him. 'Medication and therapy, that's one thing, but running? How can that help with stress?'

It's safe to say that he is not alone in going through these problems. Today, stress is the number one reason people take sick leave in Sweden, and my country is not unique. According to the American Psychological Association, 72 per cent of adult Americans experience recurring periods of high stress, and 42 per cent suffer from insomnia as a result. Just like my patient, most of them are aware that medication and therapy are two methods of treating intense stress. And just like him, many don't know that maybe the most efficient treatment is what this book is all about: physical activity. In fact, exercise and training have proven to be very impressive at both treating and preventing stress. I will now explain why this is, and how you too can literally run away from stress and anxiety.

STRESS FULFILS A FUNCTION

A good way to start coping with stress is to understand what it is and what function it fulfils. In your brain and your body, you have something called the HPA axis. The axis starts deep inside the brain in the hypothalamus (the 'H' in HPA). When the brain detects something it perceives as a threat, like, say, someone screaming at you, the hypothalamus sends a signal to the pituitary gland (the 'P') in the brain. The pituitary gland reacts to the signal by releasing a hormone into your bloodstream. which travels to your adrenal glands (the 'A'), located on top of your kidneys. They, in turn, react by releasing the stress hormone cortisol. Cortisol mobilises energy and makes the heart beat faster and harder. All this happens quickly; it only takes a second or so to go from hearing the shouting person, to having raised cortisol levels in your blood, to your heart beating faster.

Imagine that you're standing in front of a large group of colleagues and you're about to do a presentation on a project that you've worked long and hard on. You feel your heart beat faster and your mouth goes dry even though you've just had a glass of water. You wonder if anyone has noticed that your hand is trembling slightly and that the notes you're holding are shaking a little. What is happening is that your HPA axis has started to rev up and the cortisol levels in your blood are rising. Your body interprets the situation as dangerous, even though your coworkers are hardly a threat to your life. A powerful set of biological mechanisms has kicked into gear in your body, mechanisms that have been preserved through millions of years of evolution. It has now become a matter of 'fight or flight' for your body – even though in this case 'fight' means giving a good presentation, not fending off a physical attack by your colleagues. From a purely biological standpoint, there is no doubt about it: your body is preparing itself for battle.

The reason your heart is racing is simple: your muscles need more blood when you're getting ready to fight or run for your life. Rising levels of cortisol not only put the body but also the brain on high alert. Your brain becomes focused on and sensitised to the smallest change. If you hear so much as a cough in your audience, you'll react to the sound at lightning speed.

So stress fulfils a function. It makes you sharper and more focused, and while this is generally a good thing, for some the reaction becomes far too intense. Instead of getting more focused, they have trouble thinking clearly. They experience a loss of control and feel terrible distress. For them, the HPA axis seems to be spinning out of control.

The amygdala: the stress trigger

Let's backtrack a bit to see where stress actually starts. The 'warning' that your colleagues may constitute a danger doesn't come from the HPA axis but from its engine: the amygdala. The amygdala is a part of the brain that is the size of an almond, situated deep inside the temporal lobe. You have two amygdalae, one in each half of the brain. The amygdala has been preserved throughout evolution and is a part

of the brain that we share with all mammals. The reason for its continued presence is that it is incredibly important for the survival of
our species and others. There's nothing very remarkable about that –
if anything increases your chances of survival, it's having an effective
alarm system that is good at signalling when a situation is dangerous
so you can run away. And that's just what the amygdala does.

The amygdala exhibits a singular property in the biological inter-
play of stress alarm activation. Not only does it trigger the stress
function, it can also be triggered by it. Sound complicated? Here's
how it happens: the amygdala signals danger and this leads to elevated cortisol levels, which in turn activate the amygdala even *more*.
The stress feeds on itself in a vicious cycle.

If the amygdala is left to rev up the HPA axis uncontrollably,
sooner or later you will experience a full-fledged panic attack. Aside
from being extremely unpleasant, a panic attack is never a good thing
because the afflicted person often behaves irrationally. For our ancestors, panic was not compatible with survival when they came face to
face with a threatening animal out in the savanna. However, what
did increase their chances of survival was keeping a cool head and
trying to think clearly despite imminent danger.

The body has several built-in brake pedals to slow down the
stress response, preventing it from going haywire and bringing on
a panic attack. One of these is the hippocampus, often called the
memory centre of the brain. The hippocampus isn't just central to
our ability to create memories, it also works like a brake so we don't
emotionally overreact. The hippocampus can arrest the stress
response; it functions like a counterweight to the amygdala's stress
trigger. This happens continuously in your brain and not just in
stressful situations. There's always a balance between the amygdala
and the hippocampus; they pull in opposite directions from each
other. The amygdala puts the pedal to the metal, while the hippocampus slams on the brakes.

The anxiety subsides

Let's get back to your presentation, which is now over, so you can take a breather. It doesn't look like your colleagues noticed your nervousness. Nobody seems to have had an inkling that you had what felt like a chaotic storm raging inside you.

Your stress response decreases. Your body and brain lower their guard as there no longer seems to be any threat. The amygdala's activities settle down and cortisol levels drop. Your body lays down its weapons and backs off. You feel calmer.

It's important that cortisol levels fall as soon as the stressful situation blows over. A surge of cortisol is useful in a serious situation – you need that extra energy to fight or flee – but walking around with elevated cortisol for an extended period is not a good thing. This stress hormone can in fact be a poison for the brain cells in the hippocampus, since they can die off from exposure to too much cortisol. Over time – we're talking months and years here – an excess of cortisol can make the hippocampus shrink in size.

To put it mildly, this is not good news because it can lead to memory problems. After all, the hippocampus is the brain's memory centre, so many people who experience a prolonged elevated stress response, like my patient at the beginning of the chapter, experience worsening in their short-term memory. Some people who have suffered from prolonged high stress have difficulty finding words or remembering places. In fact, the latter is more likely because the hippocampus is also involved in spatial navigation.

Stress that creates stress

What is probably worse than forgetfulness is that a shrinking hippocampus becomes an increasingly weaker brake for the stress response. The hippocampus's stress brake gets worn down if the amygdala – the stress trigger – works overtime. The stress response begins to take on a life of its own when the hippocampus can no longer restrain the effects of the amygdala. Thus the amygdala – the gas pedal – speeds up, while the hippocampus – the brake – shrinks and becomes less able to slow things down. At this point we enter a vicious cycle in which stress creates more stress. This is exactly what can happen when we experience drawn-out, or chronic, periods of stress: it can literally lead to the brain breaking down. When the brains of people suffering from high stress and anxiety were examined, it was found that their hippocampi were in fact a bit smaller than average, probably due to being slowly eroded by cortisol.

A BODY THAT IS PHYSICALLY FIT COPES BETTER WITH STRESS

It is irrefutably a good idea to try to curtail the effects of cortisol on the brain if you wish to get a better handle on stress. This is where exercise enters the picture. When you go for a run, a bike ride or are otherwise active, your cortisol levels increase over the duration of the activity. This is because physical exertion is a type of stress on the body. Your muscles need more energy and oxygen to work properly, so your heart beats faster and harder to increase blood flow. Heart rate and blood pressure rise. In this case the effects of cortisol are not only normal but crucial for you to perform physically.

But your body doesn't require the same stress response after your training session is over, so your cortisol levels drop – in fact, they fall to below the level you had before you started running. If you keep up a regular running schedule, your cortisol will increase less and less during each session, and fall more and more every time you finish.

Your body's stress response will improve as you become more physically fit. Exercise teaches the body not to overreact to stress.

Now comes the really interesting part: if you continue to exercise regularly, your level of cortisol will increase less and less, even when you are under stress for reasons other than physical training. Your body's stress response, whether it be exercise or work related, will improve as you become more and more physically fit. In a nutshell: exercise teaches the body to not overreact to stress, regardless of what caused the stress.

Usually the effect is unmistakable. Maybe you've noticed, as I have, that you're less sensitive to stress during times of intense training. You might go through a highly charged, busy workday, but when you think back on it later you'll notice that you hardly felt any stress. Often this cannot be explained away with a simple 'I'm feeling a bit better overall' because you've exercised, but it is actually the result of having strengthened your body's tolerance to stress through physical activity.

CORTISOL: A 'DEATH HORMONE'?

High levels of cortisol in the blood are damaging to the hippocampus, among other things, and so cortisol has even been referred to as a 'death hormone' that wreaks havoc in the body and the brain. This moniker is unnecessarily harsh because the purpose of cortisol is not to break down the brain and cause

---

damage; it has many important responsibilities. The trouble is that our stress response, which starts with cortisol, has not evolved to contend with today's prolonged, higher-stress lifestyle.

In the environment in which human beings evolved – the savanna – stress was typically felt in short bursts. In a threatening situation, our ancestors could choose between going on the attack or running away. They didn't stay put, day after day, in front of an animal that wanted to eat them. In such situations, cortisol was a mobilising force that gave us the strength to react.

Today, most of us don't have to worry about getting eaten or killed. However, stress brought on by work deadlines, bills and house repairs is not short term but persistent. When you worry about rising interest rates and nursery pick-up times, the same response is activated as if you were standing in front of a hungry lion, except the reaction to the lion would be more intense. You could run away from the lion – or get eaten by it – and the stress would be gone. But you can't flee from your modern threats, and this means the stress never fully goes away. Fretting about your mortgage won't literally kill you, of course, but it will produce constant high levels of cortisol, which will beat up your brain in the end.

EXERCISE CALMS THE STRESS RESPONSE

The Montreal Imaging Stress Test (MIST) demonstrates how we react to stress. This is a computer-generated, timed test in which test subjects are asked to perform mental maths and mark their answers on the monitor. The result, whether right or wrong, is given immediately after each question.

Before the test, participants are informed that the average tester answers 80–90 per cent of the questions correctly. When the test begins, the computer will only register 20–45 per cent of the answers as correct, regardless of whether the subjects are right or wrong. During the test, it is revealed that the test subjects are scoring well below average. Naturally, this is extremely aggravating, which is the whole point of the test. It's not unusual for participants to drop out of the test and leave in frustration.

Stress elevates blood pressure and increases the stress hormone cortisol, which is what this test is supposed to do. In other words, it's the stress reaction that the MIST is studying, not how good the participants are at mental arithmetic. So why am I telling you about this annoying test? Because it reveals the amazing impact exercise has on stress. Scientists asked a group of healthy subjects to ride a bike for 30 minutes before they took the MIST, while another group performed gentle exercises without raising their heart rate. Afterwards, cortisol levels were lower in the subjects who had cycled, because they didn't have as strong a stress response as the others. The result was the same whether or not the participants were physically fit. Exercise calms the stress response, regardless of your physical condition.

It was also noted that the level of activity in the hippocampus (the part of the brain that acts like a brake on the stress response) was higher in the test subjects who had cycled. Their entire HPA axis was more subdued. The fact is, exercise and physical activity are truly a gift for the hippocampus. On the whole, it seems like there's nothing so beneficial for the hippocampus as being active. As you will read in Chapter 5, new cells are created in the hippocampus if you train regularly.

Allow your higher cognitive functions to nip anxiety in the bud

So the hippocampus acts like a brake on the stress response, and the brake pads can be reinforced by exercise – but the hippocampus is not

THE MIND-BODY METHOD

the only brake in your brain. The frontal lobe, which sits behind the forehead (you actually have two frontal lobes, one in each hemisphere of the brain), can also inhibit the stress response. The frontal lobe – especially its anterior (front) part, called the prefrontal cortex – is the seat of your higher cognitive functions. The ability to inhibit impulses and carry out abstract and analytical thought is situated here. During stress, the frontal lobe plays a central role in protecting you from emotionally overreacting and from acting irrationally.

When the thought, *Uh oh, we're gonna crash*, hits you during a sudden bout of turbulence on a plane, it's the amygdala, quick as a flash, that puts your body on red alert. You're in fight-or-flight mode, with a racing heart, experiencing a surge of anxiety or even a panic attack. The frontal lobe cools those feelings down with logic: *It was only an air pocket, and I've had this happen before. We didn't crash then, so why would we crash now?*

There is a constant tug of war going on between the amygdala and the frontal lobe, and not only at stressful times. Just like there's a balance between the amygdala and the hippocampus, there is a balance between the amygdala and the frontal lobe, and it can differ from person to person.

How susceptible a person is to anxiety depends to a high degree on whether their amygdala signals fear when there's no cause for it, or whether their frontal lobe is able to push back and inhibit this predilection. People whose frontal lobes can't do this tend to see danger and potential catastrophe everywhere, and walk around in a constant state of stress and foreboding.

Stress shrinks the thinking brain

Stress doesn't only shrink the hippocampus; it seems to have the same effect on the frontal lobe. Indeed, parts of the frontal lobe are smaller in individuals with very anxious personalities – it's like adding insult to injury! The longer the stress continues, the more the brain feeds on itself, and the worse the brakes work. Those suffering from chronic stress are most in need of their hippocampus and frontal lobe, which don't function optimally for them.

When the amygdala sounds the alarm at every turn and the frontal lobe is unable to balance this out, we start to overreact to stuff that is probably trivial. For example, you might think, *When I said good morning to my boss, she answered me a bit tersely. She probably doesn't like me. I must have done something wrong. I'm useless and I'll probably get fired soon.* If the frontal lobe had stepped in properly, it would have helped to gauge the situation more clearly: *My boss might have been a bit crabby this morning, but who isn't sometimes? Maybe she didn't sleep well.*

When the frontal lobe becomes more active, we seem to become calmer and less stressed; it becomes easier to withstand the anxiety generated by the amygdala. It has been shown that it is possible to increase this activity by using magnetic field stimulation on the frontal lobe, making the whole stress response simmer down.

In other words, strengthening the frontal lobe – the 'thinking' part of the brain – is crucial if you want to put a damper on stress. Since this is a book about how exercise affects your brain, you will have already figured out that physical activity will strengthen your frontal lobe and your hippocampus. In fact, the frontal lobe and the hippocampus are the two areas of the brain that are *most* helped by staying active.

What effect does training have on the frontal lobe?

How does the frontal lobe become strong when you train? Well, in lots of ways! The frontal lobe receives more blood and works better as soon as you exercise, because the blood flow in the brain increases when you're physically active. Over the long term, new blood vessels are created in the frontal lobe, improving blood and oxygen supplies, while at the same time removing more waste products.

Increased blood flow and the formation of new blood vessels are just the beginning. Today we know that regular physical activity creates a closer connection between the frontal lobe and the amygdala, which enables the frontal lobe to control the amygdala more effectively – much like a teacher has a better grip on a class when they are present in the classroom, instead of trying to oversee things from another location.

Not only that, studies show that the frontal lobe seems to grow slightly thanks to regular physical activity. This finding surprised many in the field, but it is a real discovery, not merely an assumption. When the size of the frontal lobe of healthy adults was measured at regular intervals as they took hour-long walks, the measurements indicated that the brain's outer covering, the cerebral cortex, seemed to develop in size. It seems incredible that we can measure our frontal lobe getting bigger when we take walks!

Everybody knows that working out leads to bigger muscles, but you probably weren't aware that it also develops the more sophisticated part of the brain – the part that separates us from other animals. However, there is a catch: you must hang in there and never give up! The frontal lobe won't be able to better control the amygdala overnight; it could take months. So even if training alleviates stress straight away, this is all the more reason to persevere.

You won't appreciate the full benefits for your general wellbeing and stress tolerance until after a few months of sustained exercise. But you will notice them in many ways, because the effects of lowered activity in the brain's stress response go much deeper than simply handling stress better. Research also shows that a person's self-confidence gets a boost when activity in the brain's stress response area – the HPA axis – is lowered. This is not surprising. Self-confidence is a trait that is linked to stress and anxiety, among other things.

ANATOMY OF STRESS

There is a physical connection through several nerve pathways between the frontal lobe and the amygdala. Today we believe that the better these pathways are at transmitting information, the more effectively the frontal lobe can act as a damper on the amygdala to suppress feelings of stress and anxiety.

We can look at these nerve pathways as stress and anxiety's true anatomy, the physical coupling of your rational, thinking brain with your reptilian brain. The magnitude of anxiety and stress appears to be associated with how thick these pathways are. Thick nerve pathways are better at transmitting signals between the different areas of the brain, and a thick pathway means that the frontal lobe is more effective at controlling the amygdala. In fact, modern medical technology allows us to measure the thickness of neural pathways. One of the most significant pathways between the amygdala and the frontal lobe is the uncinate fasciculus, which measures between 4 and 5cm (1.57–1.97in) in length. When examining people suffering from generalised anxiety disorder, it has been shown that their uncinate fasciculus pathway is less efficient at transmitting signals. This probably means that their frontal lobe is less able to act as a brake on their amygdala, which leads to anxiety and stress.

Are some medicines too effective?

There are medications available that provide quick relief for stress and anxiety. You've probably heard of some if not all of them: diazepam, oxazepam, Rohypnol and Xanax. The problem with these drugs is not that they are not effective because the stress and anxiety often subside soon after they have been ingested. Rather, the issue is that they work *too* well.

The brain is programmed to seek out stress relief, which is why pills that ensure immediate shelter from anxiety and bestow a sense of calm are enormously tempting. The risk is that your brain will scream for these medications once you've tried them. Furthermore, the brain tends to adapt quickly, so after only a short course of treatment the brain chemistry changes, and what provided effective relief at first is no longer enough. The dose needs to be increased to deliver the same effect, at which point you run the risk of becoming addicted.

Besides the aforementioned drugs, there is another substance that has an amazing ability to turn off feelings of stress and anxiety, but it carries with it a major risk of dependency. That substance is alcohol. Alcohol is extremely effective at quickly lowering the stress response. The fact is, there are few, if any, other substances that can compare to alcohol's power to provide relief from stress and anxiety. Anyone who has ever drunk wine or spirits when they felt anxious knows exactly what I'm talking about – a few minutes is all it takes for all the worry to vanish.

Alcohol and anxiolytic (i.e. anxiety-relieving) drugs have such similar effects that the anxiolytics have been said to give the feeling of a 'dry drunk'. The common denominator is that they both target the same system in the brain: GABA.

Your stress extinguisher

GABA is an amino acid, a molecule that the brain produces, whose purpose is to calm the brain and act as a 'fire extinguisher' to suppress the brain cells' activities. Once the brain is calmed, feelings of stress disappear. Consequently, GABA activation provides quick and effective stress relief, exactly as if you were drinking alcohol or taking anxiolytics.

What is very cool about this is that GABA isn't just activated by alcohol and pills, but also by movement – i.e. exercise. Walking yields a certain effect, but the best result comes from running or cycling. Today we know that sustained physical exertion causes GABA activity to ramp up, especially in areas of the brain situated below the cerebral cortex, and it's from there that a lot of stress originates. That GABA activity also increases there means exercise strikes at the very heart of the stress.

'Nanny neurons'

It is probably GABA that causes an interesting paradox of how exercise affects the brain. As you will see in Chapter 5, exercise leads to the creation of new brain cells, and new brain cells are like young children, in that they are extremely active. To get a three-year-old to sit calmly is just about impossible. It's the same for young brain cells, which are always active and like to send signals to other cells without any prompting from their surroundings. They do as they please. That newly born brain cells are active in the same way as newly born humans might seem kind of cute, but easily revved-up brain cells are bad news from the standpoint of stress because they can create feelings of anxiety. Anyone who experiences a lot of stress and anxiety wants to have calm brain cells that don't fire off at will.

What is remarkable is that, while training causes new, hyperactive cells to form, which should bring about more stress and anxiety, the result is that you become calm instead. This is probably because some of the new cells created through exercise are GABA cells, which instead of becoming active and out of control, help to inhibit overactivity in other newborn cells.

In American popular science articles, these GABA cells are sometimes called 'nanny neurons', reflecting their role in calming other young brain cells. The soothing influence of these nanny neurons on their environment means that the entire brain settles down. It appears that if you work out, you can create more nanny neurons to effectively inhibit activity – and therefore reduce stress levels – in the brain. 'And where do they form, these nanny neurons?' you may ask. Animal testing has shown that it's primarily in an area of the hippocampus that is important for regulating emotions and inhibiting anxiety. Even there, exercise takes aim at the heart of stress and anxiety.

WHY DO WE WORRY?

The body's built-in stress and anxiety mechanisms are there to increase our chances of survival. At the same time, today's society makes it easier for us to survive than at any other time in history. Most of us don't need to worry about dangers like not having enough food, or not having a roof over our head and we certainly don't have to worry about lurking predators, so it might seem contradictory that we still experience such high levels of stress and anxiety. We should be walking around totally calm and serene. So why aren't we?

Anxiety is the price we pay for our intelligence.

You'll find the answer in our past. Picture two groups of your ancestors on the savanna. One group is contented, taking it easy, scratching themselves between their toes and feeling that everything will turn out just fine. '*Mañana, mañana,*' they say. The other group is dissatisfied and worried. 'Do we have enough to eat? What if the weather turns bad? We may not find any more zebras or antelopes to hunt. Let's go out and fill the larder to be on the safe side.'
Which group do you think has the better odds of living a long

life? I'd place my bet on the anxious group for sure. The fact that they experience anxiety and stress helps them avoid threats and plan for the future. To see the world as dangerous – which is what anxiety means – increased their chances of survival. It is not nature playing a nasty prank on humans by making us feel stressed out and anxious; it's a survival mechanism that allowed our ancestors to forge ahead. This mechanism doesn't fit our present-day life very well, but it's still there in us whether we like it or not. And it does explain why exercise is so beneficial in combating stress and anxiety: being physically active meant hunting for food or running away from danger – in other words, doing something to survive. So when we run on the treadmill, our brain interprets this as an activity that is increasing our chances of survival, which in turn relieves our stress and anxiety.

A more philosophical spin would be to assert that our anxiety is the direct outcome of our intelligence. Having the ability to plan for the future and think about how it *might* turn out enables us to worry about things we'd prefer to avoid. That is how humans are unique. Our stress response can start now if we begin to brood about what *could* happen at work next week, without it being a real threat at this very moment. The ability to anticipate danger also means that we can plan on how to avoid it, and worry about it before it becomes a fait accompli. Anxiety is the price we pay for our intelligence.

YOUR MUSCLES ARE A STRESS TREATMENT PLANT

In a study, scientists genetically manipulated some mice so that they were born with larger than normal muscles, and they seemed to be more or less immune to stress. In experiments, every attempt to worry the animals with bright lights and loud noises failed; they appeared to have nerves of steel. What was in the muscles that protected the mice from stress? The answer is something that neutralises a metabolite called kynurenine, which is caused by stress.

The stress metabolite kynurenine can be dangerous for the brain, but with assistance from the muscles it is neutralised and thus made unable to enter the brain. It's very likely that this mechanism helped to make the mice completely impervious to stress – and the same mechanism is present in human muscles as well. This suggests that muscles are able to work as a type of treatment plant to remove damaging stress triggers. In the same way as the liver purifies blood by removing toxic substances, muscles protect the brain.

If muscles can neutralise an important stress substance, then it's easy to infer that we could become better at dealing with stress by training our muscles. While a lot points towards that conclusion – such as the muscled mice appearing resistant to stress – we don't have firm answers yet as to how big the impact would be on us humans.

Even strength is good for stress

The experiment with the muscled mice is even more exciting because this is one of the first instances where it has been shown that strength training by itself can be good for combating stress. Scientists have often focused their attention on the effects of aerobic training, but in this case it's all about our *muscles'* stress-busting potential. So can we conclude from these findings that we should rely on strength training alone to protect ourselves against stress? No, absolutely not. Even taking this into account, it's better to vary the types of physical activity you engage in, and incorporate both strength and cardiovascular training into your routine.

Exercise and physical training are fantastic antidotes to stress, maybe even the very best!

TACKLE ANXIETY FROM DIFFERENT SIDES

Are you beginning to see why training is so good for anyone suffering from stress and anxiety? It attacks the problem from several sides! Cortisol levels fall after each training session and won't rise as much the next time you're under stress. The hippocampus and the frontal lobe – the stress response's brake pedals – become stronger and more efficient at inhibiting the amygdala/anxiety engine. Activity in the brain's GABA brake system is enhanced through the creation of more nanny neurons, and the muscles' ability to neutralise the stress metabolite kynurenine increases. All this takes place simultaneously.

In reality, it's difficult to tease the different mechanisms apart and figure out how much anxiety inhibition is due to, say, decreased cortisol levels, and how much of it is because of GABA. But if we combine all the mechanisms and look at the end result – which is what is truly interesting, after all – there's no doubt that exercise and physical training are fantastic antidotes to stress, maybe even the very best!

Teenage angst no more

The number of teenagers seeking psychiatric help for stress and anxiety has risen steadily over the past few years. From a neurobiological standpoint, teenage anxiety is not surprising. The parts of the brain that dampen stress and anxiety, including the frontal lobe and prefrontal cortex, are the last to mature. They are not fully developed in a teenager; in fact, they're not completely mature until about 27–30 years of age. However, areas that *create* stress, like the amygdala, are often fully developed in a 16-year-old. The anxiety trigger being in full working order when the anxiety inhibitor is not often means the teenage years are rife with mood swings, impulsivity and anxiety.

Still, exercise can have a huge impact even on teenagers' feelings of stress and anxiety. A study was conducted in Chile on 200 healthy Year

10s hailing from a vulnerable area of Santiago, the country's capital. Chile had at the time only recently begun to suffer from Western-style diseases such as diabetes and cardiovascular disease, and the scientists wanted to see if it was possible to reverse that trend through lifestyle changes. They also wanted to investigate whether regular training would influence the youth's wellbeing and self-confidence.

At the end of the ten-week programme, the tests revealed that the training had not only produced some great fitness results, it had also improved the teenagers' confidence and sense of wellbeing. What really stood out was the effect the programme had on their stress and anxiety levels, which had had fallen significantly. The teenagers felt much calmer, less anxious and more self-confident.

Less stressed out and less cynical

Do you feel that the anxiety you may experience has nothing to do with teenage angst? In a study researching why some people have heart attacks and how stress might be involved, more than 3,000 Finnish men were asked to answer questions about their lifestyle. A summary of the results showed that the men who exercised at least twice a week had fewer issues with stress and anxiety – the same pattern that was found in Chile. Those who trained were also less prone to aggression and had a less cynical outlook on life.

So is this *solid proof* that physical activity lessens stress and anxiety? No. We don't know for sure if it was the training that made the Finnish men less stressed out and worried. Maybe it's the case that individuals who are less worried exercise more. You must use caution when drawing conclusions if you're only looking at results from the Finnish and Chilean studies. However, if you look at them together with all the other research that has been carried out, the picture becomes crystal clear: exercise has a dramatic impact on stress and anxiety throughout life, in both the young and the old.

STRESS'S DOMINANT PLACE IN THE BRAIN

It's easy to think of stress as purely negative, but of course things are not quite that simple; on the contrary, stress is essential to our ability to function. In order to learn how to better handle stress and worry – through exercise and other means – you must understand how important stress is and what it does for us.

One way to find out how important something is, remove it. So what would happen if we simply knocked out the stress response system? This was the question scientists sought to answer when they surgically removed the amygdalae from a group of monkeys. They suspected that the surgery would interfere with the animals' ability to feel fear, and to explore this hypothesis they brought in something that most people and animals feel very uncomfortable around: snakes.

Just like humans, monkeys normally have a deeply ingrained fear of snakes. But there was no trace of fear in the monkeys whose amygdalae had been removed – quite the contrary. Instead of keeping out of harm's way, they were almost too interested in the snakes, playing with them and swinging them around.

The woman who couldn't feel fear

The monkeys didn't seem to care at all about the risk they were being exposed to, but was it because they could no longer feel fear, or had the surgery damaged their brains and made them unable to understand what they were doing? Did they not realise the snakes were dangerous? Since we're unable to ask the monkeys how they perceived the situation, it would be far simpler to study people without amygdalae, but such individuals are few and far between.

This being the case, American scientists jumped at the chance to learn more about the amygdala and its effect for the stress response when they encountered a 44-year-old mother of three who suffered from Urbach–Wiethe syndrome, an extremely rare genetic disease that causes destruction in parts of the brain, including the temporal lobe. Fewer than 300 cases of Urbach–Wiethe syndrome have been reported since it first became known about in the 1920s. In this particular woman's case, only her amygdalae – one on each side of her brain – were affected.

This woman, who was of normal intelligence despite her condition, agreed to take part in a series of tests to see whether the absence of her amygdalae affected her sense of fear. The scientists brought her to a pet store to gauge her reaction to snakes, like they had done with the monkeys, and they also tested her reaction to spiders. Before this field trip, the woman asserted that she had always had an aversion to snakes and spiders. Even so, she walked right up to the terrarium, fascinated by a collection of very large snakes. They were lifted out so she could pet them, and according to the staff she didn't hesitate for a second to stroke them, even though she had been warned that the snakes could bite. The researchers asked the woman to grade her fear on an 11-point scale ranging from zero (no fear at all) to ten (most fearful). She rated playing with large, potentially life-threatening reptiles at a two.

The same thing happened when she was left to pet large, hairy tarantulas. The store's staff explained that she became almost obsessed with touching the animals without taking any precautions. In fact, they interrupted her playing with an especially large and aggressive spider because they didn't think the situation was safe any more and she ran the risk of being bitten. It didn't seem to bother her in the least that this spider was aggressive and dangerous. She was careless in a way that was reminiscent of how the monkeys had played with the snakes.

It's tempting to assume that the reason for her recklessness was her destroyed amygdalae. But before we reach this conclusion, it would be prudent, as in the case of the monkeys, to speculate whether there could have been another cause. Maybe it was only her fear of animals – even if those animals were the kind we tend to feel most anxious around – that had been affected. Perhaps she would feel frightened if confronted by something else? The next step was therefore to have her watch disturbing scenes from horror films such as *The Shining*, *The Ring* and *The Blair Witch Project* – movies that typically spook people. To ensure that the clips were creepy enough, they were first shown to a group of test subjects who were asked to rate their scariness on a scale of one to ten. Most of the clips scored between six and seven.

The film clips failed to arouse any fear in the woman, who gave them all zero. Oddly enough, however, she seemed interested in the films and found them exciting. She even asked for the title of one of them so she could rent it and finish watching it at home.

Aside from participating in experiments featuring scary animals and horror films, the woman was followed for several years. The picture that emerged was clear: it appeared that she had become utterly fearless after her amygdalae were destroyed. None of her other feelings had been affected; she could feel happy, elated or sad, depending on the circumstances. In fact, while they were showing her the film clips, the researchers saw clues that her other feelings were intact. The creepy clips were interspersed with excerpts from comedies and dramas to provoke other feelings besides fear. The woman reacted normally when watching these: she laughed at the comedy and became sad while watching a scene about an abandoned child. The absence of working amygdalae had not made her apathetic or emotionally disengaged to the point of not being able to feel anything at all; it had only taken away her ability to feel fear.

It's almost enough to make one jealous! Imagine never having to be afraid or worried, and being able to face most things in life without a care. But it wasn't so easy for the woman. Her inability to feel fear had severe repercussions. She put herself into dangerous

THE MIND-BODY METHOD

situations several times; she was robbed and threatened with both a knife and a gun. Normally these types of experiences would lead to anxiety, and most of us would be more careful and avoid areas where we've been accosted and robbed at knifepoint. However, she quickly got over what had happened and did not change her behaviour in the slightest. She lived in an economically depressed area plagued by drugs and violence, yet she went out late at night to dangerous places; despite the unsafe environment and her experiences, she did not seem to have learned to avoid perilous situations.

Our deepest fear

Was she completely immune to fear, then? No, the scientists eventually found something that made her completely freak out: dyspnoea – shortness of breath or choking. Inhaling carbon dioxide awakened a terror in her that she was previously unable to feel. If you don't breathe in enough air, the level of carbon dioxide in your body rises quickly. The brain reacts swiftly to this increase in carbon dioxide, not to the lack of oxygen. It interprets inhaling carbon dioxide as suffocation, and this fear is probably more deeply seated than any other. If you breathe in carbon dioxide, you will, sooner rather than later, be gripped by total panic. This is exactly what happened to the test subject, who for the first time in her life experienced such all-out terror that she screamed, shook and gasped for air. Her brain alerted her to a life-threatening situation, and it did so without the amygdalae.

Later, when she was asked about her experience, the woman explained that the feeling was not only the most intense she'd ever had, it was also completely new to her. So why did she feel panic at the prospect of suffocation but not when facing snakes, spiders and horror movies?

One possible explanation is that we need the amygdala to gauge external dangers, such as a snake or a person threatening us with a weapon, but not internal threats. An external occurrence must be interpreted as such – *the man in front of me with a knife is dangerous* – but the feeling of suffocation requires no explanation because that fear is deep-seated within us.

The amygdala takes charge

The examples with the monkeys and the woman illustrate how the stress response can be overridden in the brain. Moreover, they show the amygdala's role as a warning flag in the face of danger, and as the engine of the stress response. The amygdala is extremely powerful and can, quick as a flash, trigger the heart and body into action, leaving no room to think about long-term consequences. The brake pedals available to the brain – the hippocampus and the frontal lobe, for instance – which engage in deliberation and forethought, don't stand a chance in a truly dire situation. Quite simply, they are barrelled over by the amygdala.

In the environment in which we evolved – the savanna – it was critical that the amygdala be forceful. It was vitally important to be able make a lightning-quick decision if we were threatened by an animal. *Do I attack, or am I defenceless and need to run away?* In this type of situation there's no time to weigh the pros and cons for too long; take sufficient time to ponder a decision and it could be too late. Instead it's important that the amygdala takes charge and overrides the rest of the brain to react immediately, either by attacking or scampering away.

This mechanism isn't needed as much in our current society, in which we're seldom faced with life-or-death situations that require quick decisions. Now there's the risk that the amygdala will target something that isn't all that dangerous, to which we will emotionally overreact. In the mid-1990s, the American psychologist Daniel Goleman coined the term 'amygdala hijack'. This is an exaggerated emotional reaction that happens when the amygdala puts such strong emotional emphasis on an event that it's perceived as being a far worse threat than it objectively is. The amygdala 'hijacks' the brain and forces the individual into fight-or-flight mode so they no longer react rationally.

It's not enough that the emotional reaction be strong to qualify as amygdala hijacking; it also needs to happen quickly and leave you feeling remorseful afterwards. One of Goleman's prime examples was when the boxer Mike Tyson bit off Evander Holyfield's ear during a bout. Tyson acted quickly – probably more like a reflex – and seems to have met the criteria for remorse to their fullest. Aside from embarrassment, that bite cost him millions of dollars in fines and legal fees. According to Daniel Goleman, this is a typical example of amygdala hijacking.

INCREASE STRESS TOLERANCE

When we realise how powerful the brain's amygdala and stress response are, we also come to understand why we can't remove stress completely from our lives, since it's far too deeply ingrained in the brain to make that possible. We can certainly try to avoid the things that stress us out the most, but striving for a totally stress-free life would mean you would have to move out into the wild and isolate yourself! Then you'd probably stress out because you're all alone!

It's impossible to eliminate all stress from your life, but a much better goal is to try and increase your tolerance to it. That's exactly what physical activity does – it won't erase stress, but it will enable you to handle it better. Regular exercise strengthens the brain's brake pedals, so it'll take a lot more for you to enter fight-or-flight mode. Let's say you get reprimanded at work for missing a deadline. If you're fit, the likelihood of you entering panic mode, with its quickened heart rate, raised blood pressure and muddled thinking, is lessened.

Exercise increases the chance that you'll be able to cope with such a situation and not overreact physically or psychologically.

If you swap an hour at work for an hour's training from time to time, you'll get a lot more done in the rest of the day.

The last thing I want to do is to give someone with a hectic schedule a bad conscience because they don't have the time to exercise. But in my experience, if you're too stressed out to make time for regular exercise, you are probably a person that is most in need of it. So for anyone who believes they have too much on their plate to train: you will not only feel better and less stressed out if you make time to exercise, it will also be time well spent with regards to your job performance. I dare say that if you swap an hour at work for an hour's exercise from time to time, you'll get a lot more done in the rest of the day. At any rate, that's how it works for me.

Stress shows up on the scales

In case you're still not convinced that exercising is a good way to manage stress, I have one ace up my sleeve: what motivates people more than anything to begin running or visiting the gym is not that it will make them healthy, feel good or handle stress better; it is what they will see in the mirror. More than anything, wanting to lose weight or develop an athletic body is what prompts most of us to become physically active. And I've got some good news: if you increase your tolerance to stress by exercising, it will show up on the scales, too.

This is because the stress hormone cortisol prevents the body from burning fat. Having high levels of cortisol leads the body to store abdominal fat. Moreover, it increases appetite, especially for calorie-dense foods. If you're under a lot of stress and walk around with high cortisol levels, you'll risk adding more pounds around your waist and experiencing major sugar cravings. Handling your stress levels through exercise means you'll lower your cortisol levels, which over the long haul can decrease your appetite and fat storage, increase fat burning and show appreciable results on the scales and around your waist.

STRESS IS TRANSIENT, ANXIETY STICKS AROUND

You've probably experienced anxiety at one time or another – everybody does – but maybe without knowing what it was. When patients ask me to explain what anxiety is, I usually tell them that it is an overwhelming feeling of dread, of not having peace of mind, the feeling that something is wrong and you would like to 'crawl out of your own skin'.

The best way to distinguish between stress and anxiety is that stress is a reaction to something that is happening here and now that is a threat. Anxiety is to dwell on a *possible* threat, something that may or may not happen. If your boss yells at you, that is stress – a threat here and now. If you think, *Maybe my boss will yell at me tomorrow*, that is anxiety. Basically it is the same stress response – the HPA axis – causing both states of mind, but whereas stress is transient, anxiety sticks around.

So is anxiety an illness or does it fulfil a function? If we look at it from a biological perspective, we see that anxiety is a feeling of fear and dread that follows an experience we perceive as a possible threat.

Our human brains tend to present – and perceive – many things as threats because we evolved in a dangerous world. For 99.9 per cent of all generations, half of all humans died before they became teenagers. In the incredibly dangerous world that shaped the brain, it made sense to be cautious and see danger one time too many rather than one time to few. Anxiety therefore casts a wide net not because the brain is broken but because it is trying to help us survive. Anxiety can cover everything from slight discomfort to full-blown panic. It can come and go, as in the case of a panic attack, or lie low and simmer over time, as with generalised anxiety. Anxiety can be brought on by traumatic memories, as with post-traumatic stress disorder, or flare up in social settings, as with social phobia. Although only a few anxiety disorders are officially recognised, in reality there are as many variations of anxiety as there are people.

But is anxiety dangerous? Many who have experienced intense anxiety due to panic attacks believe it is. Some even fear they are going to die. Many think they are alone in their plight. They are all mistaken. Even if anxiety is unpleasant, it is neither dangerous nor rare. Your heart will not stop if you are anxious, even if it feels like it might. And the anxiety sufferer is *not* alone; anxiety is both a common and a benign reaction that most of us experience to different degrees, and that at times can go completely overboard for some of us. Anxiety is both normal and hellish at the same time. If you have severe problems with it, you should seek help. Seeking help is a sign of strength.

TRAINING OR RELAXATION?

As you learn more about the research around how exercise affects stress, it becomes obvious that everybody who sometimes suffers from stress – children and adults alike – ought to try physical exercise in one form or another. This doesn't mean you should disregard relaxation, meditation, mindfulness or yoga, which also might be good, but if you don't exercise, you might miss out on perhaps the most effective way to handle stress and anxiety. And if you have to choose between training and, for example, relaxation, exercise is the better choice. If everybody started being a bit more physically active – just a bit, I'm not talking about running a marathon – it would have mind-boggling consequences on the stress levels people are living with today. Fewer people would need psychiatric help and nearly everybody, whether they suffer from stress or not, would feel so much better.

Unconscious fear

We can inquire about what causes anxiety. We know sufferers have an overactive and easily triggered amygdala that signals danger without any threat being present; they see potential catastrophes on every street corner without being conscious of it. In one study, individuals were tested for anxiety by being shown pictures of angry and neutral faces for just two-hundredths of a second. Most were not aware they had seen a face and the ones who did see it could not tell the expression. But even though the face flashed past too quickly for anybody to pick out an expression, anxiety-ridden people reacted differently to the pictures.

When examining the individuals' brains using MRI, the amygdalae of anxiety sufferers were visibly more easily activated when they looked at pictures of angry faces. Moreover, the more significant the anxiety issue, the quicker the amygdala was fired up by the angry faces, even though the viewer was not conscious of what they were seeing! For neutral facial expressions, which cannot be interpreted as a threat, there was no discernible difference between the amygdala's reaction in healthy people and that of those suffering from an anxiety disorder. People suffering from high anxiety have an amygdala that's always in the starting blocks, ready to go, ready to signal danger, and in doing so it activates the body's stress response.

Exercise your anxiety away

It's often difficult to separate stress from anxiety. After all, it's all part of the same system (including the HPA axis and the amygdala) that is active in both stress and anxiety. Physical exercise, as you have seen earlier, has an amazing effect on stress, which is why it is also a great way to treat anxiety.

In one study, American students suffering from anxiety drew lots to either walk or run for 20 minutes a few times a week over the course of two weeks – hardly a gruelling training regimen either way. Anxiety levels fell for both the walkers and the runners, and their anxiety wasn't just lower after exercise; it stayed low over the next 24 hours, and the effect lasted an entire week. So who experienced the highest impact on their anxiety levels? The runners. More effort is obviously better if you wish to lower your anxiety.

This isn't surprising if you think about it. Anxiety is caused by overactivity in the brain's stress response and an amygdala signalling danger where there is none. Exercise strengthens the brain's brake pedals against worry, and the frontal lobe and hippocampus become better at calming the amygdala, thereby preventing anxiety.

Anxiety: a learning problem

In principle, everyone would experience high anxiety if they were exposed to a life-threatening situation; on the other hand, not everyone becomes overwhelmed by anxiety when doing something like stepping onto a tube train. I once had a patient who suffered a severe panic attack, complete with racing heart and trouble breathing, when taking the underground. Her terror was so strong that she was convinced she was going to die. If you've ever experienced this, you'd know that this would be the last thing that anyone would want to repeat. And that is precisely why this woman, following that attack, has chosen to travel exclusively by bus. She knows that the underground is not dangerous; it's that her brain misinterpreted the situation – and the mechanisms that misread the event were so powerful they overrode her 'thinking brain'.

The amygdala, as you have seen, is so powerful that it can over-rule the brain. Moreover, it is excellent at making sure we remember threatening situations very well. This is logical from the point of view of survival. We are hard-wired to remember distinctly what turned out to be unpleasant or dangerous so we can avoid it in the future. From an evolutionary perspective, it's not as critical to remember the five beautiful clearings in the woods as it is to remember where the wolf charged at us. Because of this, negative memories take precedence.

But the fact that memories connected to fear are so vivid means they can become a hindrance when you wish to treat anxiety disorders such as panic attacks. For anyone who has experienced a panic attack on a tube train, even walking past the entrance can be enough to tell the amygdala to trigger the stress response and the HPA axis. Even if this person eventually overcomes their fear and dares to take the tube, it can take a long time before they feel OK doing so. The unpleasant memory is so strong that it blanks out all the memories of uneventful tube journeys that didn't feature panic attacks.

Considered this way, you can view anxiety disorders as a learning problem. The brain can't learn that something is not dangerous. So, if it is programmed to clearly retain the memory of what is threatening, how can we ever be free of anxiety and worry? The solution is to slowly and patiently build up new memories in which, for example, the tube journey is not full of panic or apprehension. This is exactly what takes place during cognitive behavioural therapy, when a patient is gradually introduced to more of what causes their anxiety in order to learn that it isn't dangerous. This memory slowly morphs from an anxiety-inducing misinterpretation into something the brain considers neutral and non-threatening.

Exercise teaches the brain that a raised heart rate and blood pressure don't necessarily mean anxiety and panic, but that positive feelings may ensue.

Increased heart rate doesn't have to mean anxiety

This leads us to another reason why exercise is so beneficial in treating anxiety. Heart rate and blood pressure increase in tandem with symptoms of high anxiety. The heart beats faster and harder and the body prepares itself for fight or flight, for something negative to happen. But then the heart also beats faster and harder if you're out jogging, and your exercise session doesn't end in some kind of unpleasant episode. Instead you feel calm when the run is over, and you're rewarded with surges of endorphins and dopamine. Exercise teaches the brain that a raised heart rate and blood pressure don't necessarily mean anxiety and panic, but that positive feelings may ensue.

This is exactly what was observed in the anxiety-ridden American students who were asked to walk and run. Those who ran were no longer nervous about their increased heart rate. Before, they had equated a racing heart with an imminent anxiety attack, but their body had since made the adjustment that an elevated rate was not a threat but the very opposite – that it could be a positive thing. This effect was not seen in those who walked; for them, the brain still appeared to misinterpret the quicker heart rate as dangerous. This underscores the importance of moving more intensely if you wish to overcome anxiety and worry.

It was long believed that those experiencing a lot of anxiety and worry should avoid training. Today we know that nothing could be further from the truth. Indeed, they are the ones who are most in need of exercise. However, I must warn you that it's important to start out carefully if you have ever suffered a panic attack. Intense training can be risky because the brain could misinterpret it as an impending crisis and cause an attack in someone who isn't ready. For that reason, it's better to start out slowly and ramp up the effort gradually.

Exercise is the opposite of stress

When you look closely at research on physical activity and stress, a clear pattern emerges: stress and physical training seem to have almost opposite effects on the brain. Increased stress – i.e. having high levels of the stress hormone cortisol – impedes brain cells' ability to communicate with one another, whereas training boosts that ability. Stress decreases the brain's ability to change (its plasticity), while training increases it. Higher stress applies the brake to the transfer of information from short-term memory to long-term memory, while training releases it. And so on. For one biological mechanism after another, it appears that stress and exercise yield the exact opposite effects. This literally makes exercise and physical activity an antidote to stress and anxiety!

TRAIN AND PREVENT PANIC ATTACKS

There are some people who will do just about anything to help advance the cause of research. I would like to introduce the 12 bravest test subjects I know of. They all agreed to receive an injection of the substance cholecystokinin tetrapeptide 4 (CCK-4), which has an extremely nasty effect: it can bring on a panic attack, complete with breathing difficulties and a racing heart. The feeling is so strong that some people believe they're going to die. This is what happened to six of the twelve participants; they broke out in a cold sweat, had trouble breathing and were overcome by paralysing fear, even though none of them had ever suffered panic attacks before.

This test was then repeated – amazingly the test subjects volunteered again – but with a big difference: the participants exercised quite intensely (at 70 per cent of maximum capacity) for 30 minutes prior to getting their CCK-4 injection. Something extraordinary happened: only one test subject experienced a panic attack. Evidently the training showed immediate results and decreased the likelihood of having such an episode.

Agreeing to be injected with a panic-inducing substance is undeniably brave, but another test group showed even more guts. This group had experienced panic attacks before and knew how horrible they could be, and yet they consented to go through yet another one thanks to CCK-4. Despite only getting half a dose compared to the healthy group, nine people in the test group had a panic attack. But as with the healthy group, the number of panic attacks declined when the test subjects were told to exercise beforehand. Only four out of the twelve subjects experienced a panic attack; furthermore, they felt that the event was less severe than those they had experienced before.

Thus training has a preventive effect on panic attacks, both in prior sufferers and in those who have never experienced one. So if exercise works in such severe cases of anxiety, it should definitely help with the garden-variety anxiety so many of us grapple with today.

THE RIGHT PRESCRIPTION TO RID YOURSELF OF STRESS AND ANXIETY

What is the best way to train to rid yourself of stress and anxiety? Based on research, there is no programme that specifies exactly how intensely and for how long you should move your body to lower your stress level and prevent anxiety, and everyone responds differently to exercise. However, there are some concrete tips, based on scientific research, that you can follow:

- Focus on cardiovascular training at the onset. It appears that aerobic training is more beneficial than weight training from a stress-relief standpoint. Work out for at least 20 minutes; try to make it 30–45 minutes if you have the stamina.
- Make exercise a habit, because the results will only get better as you continue. It takes time for the hippocampus and the frontal lobe – two of the brain's stress brakes – to become stronger.
- Try to get your heart rate up at least two to three times a week. Your body will then learn that a faster heartbeat is not a cause for fear, but a state of being that brings about positive changes. This is especially important if you suffer from more serious anxiety problems and panic attacks.
- Aim to reach the point of fatigue once a week – with interval training, for example. This is extremely effective in combating anxiety. However, start out carefully and build up slowly if you have suffered panic attacks or serious bouts of worry in the past, otherwise you could bring on an anxious reaction.

- If for some reason you can't or won't raise your heart rate, just go for a walk. This also has an anxiety-suppressing effect, though it's not quite as strong as if you were to exercise more briskly.

CHAPTER 3

IMPROVED CONCENTRATION

Strength of mind is exercise, not rest.

ALEXANDER POPE

DO YOU SOMETIMES find it hard to focus? If so, welcome to the club! In today's world of information overload, where mobile phones, tablets and computers jostle for our attention, it's virtually impossible not to get distracted. Being engrossed in a task, captivated by it to the point where time stands still, is so rare – for me at least – that I would consider it a luxury.

Fixing our flagging attention has become big business. There is a steady stream of self-help books, food supplements and home remedies that are supposed to improve our powers of concentration, but most of them have no proven merit whatsoever.

In truth, there is a remedy that not only helps but makes a huge difference; it is, once again, physical activity. It is only over the past few years that we've been able to show that we become more focused – and otherwise more alert – through exercise, and we've become knowledgeable about what happens inside the brain.

FOCUS ON ONE THING

Let's go back and start from the beginning. To see if anything can boost our powers of focus, we must be able to measure this power – so how can it be done? Is it enough to simply ask someone if they're feeling focused? In science, you would want to have a more objective measure. Enter the Eriksen flanker task, an exercise that uses five arrows on a monitor. The task requires the test subject to indicate in which direction the middle arrow is pointing, as quickly as possible. Occasionally all the arrows go in the same direction (<<<<<), which makes things easy, but sometimes the middle arrow points in one direction and the others go in the other direction (>><>>), so the trick is to ignore all the arrows except the middle one. The test is fast-paced; the arrows are only shown for two seconds. To quickly single out and focus on only part of what you see and ignore the rest of the information – in this case, the surrounding arrows – the brain needs to block out irrelevant information. This is called 'selective attention'.

This type of test might seem trivial, but it is in fact an accurate way to measure our ability to zero in on one thing and not become distracted by our surroundings. Selective attention is an important part of our ability to focus and an extremely valuable trait in today's world. Imagine a day at the office: you're on the computer while two of your colleagues are chatting away, and someone else is attacking the printer. The phone pings with incoming texts and emails. You're trying to get your work done amid all of this, so it's important that you concentrate and not be sidetracked by all the buzz around you. This is selective attention, which is what the Eriksen flanker task measures.

That exercise can affect selective attention and focus became obvious when a group of people were given the Eriksen flanker task and had their physical fitness tested at the same time. The experiment indicated that the participants who were fit did better on the test – i.e. they had better selective attention. But it doesn't end there. The subjects' brains were also examined by MRI during the test, and it was noted that areas of the parietal lobe and the frontal lobe – parts of the brain that are vital to our ability to focus – were more active in the subjects who were in good shape. Activity in the areas important for focus was higher in that sample of testers.

Be that as it may, we can't make too much of this information since we cannot say for sure that better selective attention is due to people's fitness. It could be the case that people who can concentrate harder tend to enjoy exercise and are therefore fitter, rather than the other way around. Consequently, the next step was to look at new test subjects, who were training to increase their fitness, to see if this would improve their selective attention. The participants were split into two groups. One group met three times a week to walk on a treadmill for 45 minutes. The other group performed low-impact stretching and yoga exercises; they did this as many times and for the same duration as the walking group, with one key difference: they did not raise their heart rate.

Six months later, it was time to see if either group had improved at the Eriksen flanker task and to check for any noticeable differences in the subjects' brains. Sure enough, there were differences! The walkers had not only improved their selective attention and did better on the test, but the activity in the parts of the frontal and parietal lobes responsible for selective attention showed changes, too. This effect was only seen in the participants who walked. Engaging in physical activity as simple and uncomplicated as regular walking for six months didn't simply improve selective attention, it produced a measurable effect on the brain.

Why is this the case? One possible explanation is that walking might have increased the number of connections between brain cells in the frontal lobe, which made it easier for the brain to recruit additional mental capacity in these areas when the intellectual load became high. Like a car shifting into a higher gear, the brain makes use of an extra 'focus gear' to stay on track when there's a lot of distraction around. We become more adept at filtering out what is unimportant. The study's authors could not have been any clearer when they stated that the end results showed 'a brain that is more efficient, has better plasticity, and better adaptive capacity'.

But how does exercise achieve this effect, and how can you exercise to improve your focus? In this instance the test subjects walked, but is running, cycling or swimming better? And for how long? The answer can be found in research into how exercise affects a specific condition that impacts the ability to concentrate. The number of diagnoses of this condition have mushroomed over the past few years, and we all see traces of it in ourselves to a greater or lesser degree: attention deficit hyperactivity disorder (ADHD).

The ADHD epidemic

A Google search for ADHD brings up 1,300,000,000 (yes, 1.3 *billion*) results. ADHD has become our era's most recognised and discussed medical problem. It is also the diagnosis that has increased the most, by a wide margin. Around the turn of the millennium, *Time* magazine warned that too many children were being prescribed medication for ADHD and asked the controversial question: 'Do we drug our children?' At the time, between 4 and 5 per cent of all American children and adolescents had been diagnosed with ADHD. Twenty years later, these numbers look tame. Almost 10 per cent of children and teenagers in the US – more than 6,000,000 kids – have been diagnosed with ADHD. This increase has been so explosive that it has often been hard at first to find ADHD medication. The demand has been so huge that pharmaceutical companies couldn't keep up. Sweden is trailing the US by a few years, although the number of diagnoses has risen sharply, from 1 per cent at the beginning of 2000 to closer to 8 per cent in 2023. (In the UK, childhood ADHD diagnoses have risen from 1 to 3.5 per cent in the same time span.)

We're all somewhere along the ADHD spectrum

ADHD means that you have difficulties in three areas: concentration, impulsivity and hyperactivity – like the boy in class who could never sit still, who bounced around like a pinball and paid attention to everything except what the teacher was writing on the blackboard. He acted on every little whim. There's no doubt he had trouble concentrating and that he was impulsive and hyperactive – he ticked the three boxes for an ADHD diagnosis. But do we have to be like him to be suffering from ADHD? We all have difficulty focusing from time to time, but that doesn't mean we all have ADHD. Concentration is affected by things such as sleep, stress, time of day and what's happening around us.

Furthermore, concentration can vary over long periods of time; the same goes for impulsivity and hyperactivity. So where do we draw the line between run-of-the-mill concentration problems and ADHD? To put it mildly, that's not easy to figure out.

There are no blood tests or X-rays to tell you if you have ADHD. Instead, you must meet the criteria on a checklist. Other than having trouble with concentration, impulse control and hyperactivity, these problems must also affect your everyday life. Having problems at school is not enough, because that could be due to a poor academic environment. The problems should also be apparent at home or in the workplace. The difficulties should also be obvious from as early as childhood. ADHD isn't something you catch; it's a lifelong issue.

Being diagnosed with ADHD requires that you have serious problems with concentration and impulse control. What does 'serious problems' mean exactly? If you've had issues with concentration but were still able to graduate from university, does that suggest you don't have ADHD? At the risk of repeating myself here, there are no simple answers to these questions. ADHD is, unlike many other medical diagnoses, a vast grey area. In no way am I comparing apples to oranges, but it's impossible to 'have a little bit of HIV'; either you're infected or you're not. But you can suffer from 'a little bit of ADHD'. The diagnosis is neither black nor white but deals with qualities that are typically variable among us human beings. We're all somewhere along the ADHD spectrum and we all exhibit the characteristics for the diagnosis to a greater or lesser degree. Some of us have more of them than others.

THE REWARD SYSTEM IS THE BRAIN'S ENGINE

Keeping in mind that ADHD includes problems many of us grapple with, it's wise to wonder if there's anything, aside from medication, that can help. Even people with concentration problems don't necessarily go on to be diagnosed with ADHD. This is where exercise enters the picture. The connection between physical activity and concentration begins in an unexpected place, namely in the area that makes you feel good when you eat tasty food, or socialise with friends, or get praise at work: your brain's reward system.

The reward system is incredibly powerful and can be compared to an engine that pushes us towards certain behaviours. There are several parts of the brain that are important for reward, but the one we typically refer to when we say 'reward centre' is the nucleus accumbens, a pea-sized cluster of brain cells connected to many other parts of the brain. This is where you get your 'reward', your feeling of pleasure. The nucleus accumbens is what drives you. There are several substances that act as messengers between brain cells, known in scientific parlance as neurotransmitters, the best known of which is dopamine. Certain behaviours, such as eating good food, socialising with others, being physically active and having sex, increase levels of dopamine in the nucleus accumbens. This spike of dopamine gives you a positive feeling that makes you want to repeat those behaviours, so your brain pushes you to engage in them. But why does your brain want you to eat, socialise, be physically active and have sex? The answer is simple: from an evolutionary perspective, these behaviours increase your chances of surviving and transmitting your genes to the next generation.

If there is a purely biological meaning of life, it is to survive and transmit your genes – i.e. have children – and the brain is hard-wired with that as its North Star. You need food to survive. Socialising with others is crucial for the survival of a herd animal like a human. Having sex increases the likelihood of transmitting your genes through procreation.

Our ancestors didn't run for the fun of it, or for weight control, but because it increased their chances of survival. That's why we also benefit from being physically active.

So what about exercise – why does that make us feel good? Probably because when our ancestors ran they usually did so when they were hunting, escaping from predators or finding new places to settle – activities that promoted survival and were consequently rewarded by the brain. Unlike us, our ancestors didn't run for the fun of it, or for weight control, but because it increased their chances of survival. That's why we also benefit from being physically active, even today.

No concentration without reward

By rewarding behaviours with good feelings, the nucleus accumbens steers you towards actions that increase your chances of surviving and transmitting your genes. But the reward system isn't just there to make you feel warm and fuzzy, it is also central to your ability to concentrate. The nucleus accumbens isn't 'turned off' most the time, only turning on when you eat a good meal, have sex or find out that you've won the lottery. It's always active and providing feedback to the rest of your brain about whether what you're doing is worth continuing with or not. Let's say you're watching TV. If your nucleus accumbens isn't stimulated enough by the programme – i.e. if your dopamine levels aren't elevated – your attention will shift and you'll look elsewhere for a hit of dopamine – maybe your mobile phone. If you constantly lose focus and scan your surroundings for something interesting, you'll be perceived as restless and distracted.

Today we know that the reward system appears to be different from person to person. In some it's finely tuned as soon as they're born, while in others it works less well. Many, but not all, people with significant concentration issues have a reward system that runs differently. What increases dopamine levels for most of us isn't enough for them.

Their reward system requires more stimuli to become active, and that has major consequences. A reward system that is underactivated will lead the person to constantly change their focus and look for something that will give them a larger thrill. They opt for whatever delivers the best, most immediate pleasurable experience and ignore what is good for them in the long run. They have trouble setting up and following long-term goals and are interrupted by distractions large and small. They become careless, impulsive and hyperactive.

It has been shown that the nucleus accumbens isn't as active when a person with significant concentration problems – someone with ADHD, for instance – is exposed to what would normally be considered a reward. It seems more potent rewards are needed to activate their reward centre.

WORLD CHAMPION OF BAD DECISIONS

I have met hundreds of patients with ADHD. One of them, a 44-year-old man, described his symptoms in a clearer way than a medical textbook ever could:

If there were such a thing, I would probably have been crowned world champion of bad decision-making. I have always chosen what works for me in the present moment, damn the long-term consequences. I could never sit still in school, and had to be in a special education class where everyone behaved much like I did. My grades were awful, and I ended up running with a bad crowd and experimenting with drugs by the time I was 13. I quite quickly discovered amphetamines, which became my drug of choice. What made other people hyper had a calming effect on me.

Naturally, the combination of drugs and risk taking was a recipe for disaster, and as my drug addiction become more expensive, my criminal activities turned serious. It all ended with a spell in prison.

When I told my story to the doctor at the prison, he diagnosed me with ADHD. After I was put on medication I could suddenly focus, my life got clearer and I began to get things done. It became easier to function every day, and to socialise with friends; I could be present and not feel perpetually out of it, as if I were somewhere else.

This man's story is not just a crystal-clear description of ADHD, it is typical; I've heard similar accounts from many other patients. While each one of them suffered great strife due to a lack of concentration and impulse control, not many of them became addicts or criminals. What is striking is that this man looked markedly well trained and was very fit. He had made working out a priority for his entire life despite his otherwise self-destructive ways because the only time he would feel calm and focused was after exhausting himself physically: 'Then I'd be like everyone else and could listen to others without being distracted by everything around me. Now I realise that, throughout my life, working out has been a type of ADHD medication.'

Too few receptors in the reward centre

Nowadays we've begun to understand, at the molecular level, why there are differences between the reward centres of different people. For dopamine to have an effect in the reward centre and make you feel good, it must be able to bind to a receptor on the surface of a brain cell. The dopamine plugs into the receptor, which sets off a reaction in the brain cell that makes you feel pleasure. However, if there are no receptors for the dopamine to plug into, the reaction does not occur. Interestingly, it looks like people with ADHD have fewer dopamine receptors in their reward centre. This means that their reward system doesn't work well, and they require greater rewards to be responsive.

This means there are some people whose brain, from the onset, demands more stimulation to activate the reward centre. What someone with a 'normal' reward centre deems sufficiently interesting to keep their attention – a work task, a TV series or what the teacher is writing on the blackboard – is not adequate for someone with ADHD; it doesn't create enough activity in their reward centre. This person becomes bored, subconsciously attempts to find further stimulation in some other way and consequently loses their concentration. Concentrating on work or on what the teacher is writing becomes impossible. Then again, all of us are perched somewhere on the ADHD spectrum. Most of us don't have a reward system that is hypersensitive or a system with such low activity that it requires huge amounts of stimulation. Instead, most of us find ourselves somewhere in the middle of these extremes.

Consciousness and attention

The greatest mystery of the brain, and perhaps of all scientific mysteries, is how this collection of cells inside the cranium, weighing only slightly more than a kilogram (2.2lb), becomes conscious. How it turns into *you*. It was long considered frivolous to even *attempt* to understand consciousness – a bit like researching the meaning of life. But today's scientific research into the conscious mind is as far from frivolous as you can get. Recent medical discoveries have provided us with a whole new set of tools for studying consciousness. It's not just a matter of interest to neuroscientists; physicists, psychologists and philosophers are also trying their best to figure out how some cells – because that's what our bodies and brains are made of, after all – can become aware of their own existence. How can they comprehend how they are built and what place they occupy in the space–time continuum?

So where has this research led us? Where *is* our consciousness located? The short answer is, we don't know. Some of history's great thinkers have put forth their ideas. Plato, for instance, didn't believe that our mortal body could create consciousness. Polymath Leonardo da Vinci leaned towards the theory that consciousness was most likely connected to the brain but located in its fluid-filled cavities, i.e. the cerebral ventricles. The philosopher René Descartes suggested that our consciousness was situated in the pineal gland, a small gland in the brain that we now know secretes the hormone melatonin, which regulates sleep and wakefulness.

No disrespect intended, but modern neurological research has proven the aforementioned geniuses to be mistaken. Today, no one disputes the fact that our consciousness is *in fact* created in the brain, and that it is not in one singular location. Our senses of smell, sight and hearing all have specific centres, but there isn't a lone consciousness centre. Instead, it seems that many areas in the cerebral cortex make up and work together as an advanced network, and that consciousness is the result of collaboration between the frontal and temporal lobes, along with the centres for sensory impressions (like the sight and hearing centres).

The thalamus is a part of the brain that acts like a junction. It is situated in the brain like the hub on a bicycle's wheel, from which the spokes radiate out. To illustrate: information is brought into the thalamus from the brain's different areas, like the centres for sensory impressions, and from there it is spread out to other areas through the advanced network. It is within this network that we believe our experience of consciousness is created.

What does all this have to do with concentration? Well, consciousness isn't just fascinating from a philosophical and scientific point of view, it is also closely connected to our ability to pay attention and focus. Your brain is constantly filled to bursting with activity; information from different areas is competing for a place in your consciousness. You're fed sensory information about what position your legs and arms are currently in, whether the room is warm or cold, if you're feeling pain, and what you're seeing and hearing right now, which could be the words in this sentence or a car beeping out in the street. Your consciousness sifts through all of this and decides what your brain should concentrate on – hopefully it's this sentence! – and what is unimportant.

Dopamine turns off the din

Let's say you're in a coffee shop and you're reading a book. First, you're aware of the murmur of the people in the background, but that sound slowly recedes and you can concentrate on what you're reading. But even though you're no longer listening to the voices, your brain still registers what is being said. If someone in the coffee shop says your name, you'll react even though you weren't actively listening. Part of your brain must be hearing without you being aware of it, so you'll turn your attention in that direction. Obviously this happens automatically. The brain possesses the amazing ability to process huge numbers of impressions without our being aware of this, and it can sound the alarm and focus our attention on what it deems important.

We need dopamine to turn down the din that our sensory centres bombard us with, and to direct our attention towards whatever we are doing. Dopamine has considerably more responsibilities than just being a 'reward molecule'; it is also critical for concentration. Lacking dopamine can lead us to become distracted by background noise, unfocused and jittery. We all go through this sometimes; we feel unsettled, jumpy and absentminded, especially if we've slept badly or we've drunk alcohol the night before.

Oddly enough, there's another kind of din in your head, a kind of inbuilt hum that doesn't originate in the sensory centres. It's something we all experience and it doesn't mean we're hearing things. It's probably caused by brain cells activating spontaneously from time to time. This happens continuously, but you probably don't notice it because dopamine filters it out.

However, without a finely tuned dopamine system, that interior noise – like the din from the sensory centres – can become bothersome. Neurological tests have shown that people with ADHD have a louder inbuilt hum than people without ADHD, which impairs their ability to concentrate. The more interior noise there is, the worse the focus.

It's interesting to notice that if dopamine levels increase, the interior, non-stimulus-driven thrum will stop. Both the noise from your sensory centres (the din in the cafe, for example) and the inbuilt hum call it quits. It's like turning down the irritating background sound of static; dopamine lowers the volume and silences the hiss. There's no more disturbance and it becomes easier to focus.

THE NATURAL CONCENTRATION MEDICATION

Low or incorrectly regulated dopamine levels can cause a din that keeps the dopamine system insufficiently activated which makes it difficult to concentrate. Therefore, the obvious next step is to try and treat the lack of focus and to increase and stabilise dopamine levels through artificial means. That's the mechanism behind most ADHD medications: they boost dopamine levels, which in turn lead to improved focus. Many ADHD sufferers claim that their existence becomes sharper and clearer after taking medication, which probably stems from the fact that the hum in their brain – internal and external – has been silenced. However, not everyone who goes on medication experiences this. Also, not everyone wants to take medication. Add to this all the people who occasionally have trouble concentrating without having full-blown ADHD. Is there any other way to boost dopamine levels without resorting to pharmaceuticals? There is: move your body.

Possibly the most important reason why exercise is good for concentration – whether you suffer from ADHD or not – is because physical activity raises dopamine levels and fine-tunes the systems for attention and reward. Today we know that dopamine levels increase *after* you've been physically active. They rise a few minutes after a training session, and they remain raised, often for several hours. This makes you feel sharp, focused and calm after exercising. You feel better and it's easier for you to focus. The hum is hushed.

Exercise is effective medicine for improving concentration with no side effects whatsoever.

It appears that dopamine levels rise higher the more strenuous the exercise, so from dopamine's standpoint, going for a run is better than going for a walk. This is all the more reason why you shouldn't give up if you don't feel better right away, or if your focus has not improved after the first run or bike ride, because the more you train, the more dopamine you'll get. The brain seems to increase dopamine more and more with each training session, so the more often you run the trail or cycle that loop, the greater your dopamine reward. This means you'll feel better every time you complete a session, since the dopamine also affects your sense of wellbeing, and your concentration improves even more. In other words, exercise is effective medicine for improving concentration with no side effects whatsoever. Furthermore, its effect is enhanced the longer you continue.

Brain boss

Dopamine has many important effects on the frontal lobe. It's the frontal lobe, especially its anterior part – the prefrontal cortex – that make conscious decisions in the brain. The prefrontal cortex is the brain's boss and its most developed area. The ability to set and follow through with long-term goals, instead of simply acting on impulse, is found here. The same is true for our advanced cognitive functions – those that separate us from other animals – such as abstract, mathematical and logical thinking.

The frontal lobe is also largely responsible for controlling our ability to concentrate. Simply put, we have a lot of turbulence in the deeper reaches of the brain. The frontal lobe suppresses this commotion and behaves like a filter that removes the noise and allows us to focus.

The ability to wait for reward

How the frontal lobe works plays a pivotal role in how our life will turn out. In the 1970s, professor of psychology Walter Mischel revealed that children's ability to delay a reward – a function that exists primarily in the frontal lobe – can predict their future personality profile. Mischel's test (which he filmed) of delayed gratification involved four-year-old children who had to choose between enjoying a marshmallow right away or having two if they waited 15 minutes to get them.

Most of the kids found the temptation too great and could only wait 2–3 minutes before eating the treat. Some children could restrain themselves a little longer; some even managed to hold out for the entire 15 minutes in order to get the two marshmallows.

Mischel followed these test subjects for several decades and noted that those who could delay gratification, on average, did better academically and reached higher education levels as adults. They encountered fewer problems with alcohol abuse, drugs and obesity. They also handled stress better. An interpretation of this is that the variations in how people's frontal lobes function are visible early in life and have lifelong consequences.

To control the impulse to eat the marshmallow requires a great deal of discipline from a 4-year-old child (this is true for adults, too), which is a function that is connected to concentration. An important reason why some children do better on the test than others is because

THE MIND-BODY METHOD

they are better able to focus on the future reward and thus succeed in zeroing in on that future reward. In the film, you can see some children straining to breaking point, kicking frantically against the chair in front of them to distract themselves. When those who could wait were asked how they did it, they replied that they thought intensely about the fact that they would soon get two marshmallows.

This kind of concentration and ability to delay gratification are executive functions also known as 'cognitive control', which are part of what Walter Mischel calls the brain's 'cooling system'. The Nobel Prize laureate Daniel Kahneman calls it 'System 2' – the brain's slower, more deliberate system. Other scientists and authors throughout history have used different designations, but they all basically refer to the same thing: the system we have for our higher thinking that keeps a lid on impulses and has its origin in the frontal lobe and prefrontal cortex. And it's a system that is strengthened in many ways by being physically active.

It is not your brain that controls you – it is you who control your brain through your actions.

You control your brain, not the other way around

As you saw earlier in Chapter 2, the frontal lobe (I use the singular even though we have two frontal lobes) is a part of the brain that is strengthened the most by physical exercise. The frontal lobe of a person who works out regularly becomes better connected to other parts of the brain, which is critical for its ability to influence and control the rest of the brain. New blood vessels are also created in the frontal lobe in people who are physically active, which allows for better blood supply and removal of waste products. The processes that turn your walks or runs into a stronger frontal lobe are powerful but not immediate. You won't notice anything different after one loop around the track but after several months of regular activity.

Because the frontal lobe is changeable and malleable, Walter Mischel is careful to stress that the marshmallow test does not mean that those who can't resist temptation are condemned to have problems later in life. You can practise resisting temptation, and physical activity is probably a very important step in doing this. It is not your brain that controls you – it is you who control your brain through your actions. If you want to ensure the best possible conditions for yourself, staying physically active is not the only important thing, but it is more important than most people think.

CHILDREN WITH ADHD NEED EXERCISE AND PLAY

When you come to terms with how important the frontal lobe and dopamine are for concentration – and how they are influenced by exercise – you realise that, at least in theory, it should be possible to treat ADHD with physical training. But as you know, theory and practice don't always converge, so what does the research tell us? Is exercise so effective in sharpening our concentration that we can even use it to treat ADHD?

A group of scientists decided to explore this question by using 17 children as test subjects, all of whom exhibited such hyperactive behaviour that they were at risk of being diagnosed with ADHD. Over the course of eight weeks, the kids enjoyed extra physical activity in the form of play before the start of the school day. The goal was to get them out of breath and raise their heart rate. At the end of those eight weeks, the kids performed a battery of tests that measured their ability to concentrate and socialise with other children. Additionally, the kids' parents and teachers were asked if they had noticed any progress.

Did all this activity have any effect? It did. According to the parents, teachers, researchers and instructors, more than two-thirds of the children became more focused. Progress was especially noted in 'response inhibition', i.e. the ability to suppress actions and not act impulsively on every little thing, which tends to be very difficult for children with ADHD.

As little as five minutes of exercise improved concentration and lessened ADHD symptoms in children.

Despite these promising results, it couldn't be ignored that this was a very small study, so the same test was repeated on over 200 children, half of whom were at high risk of being diagnosed with ADHD. Over the course of 12 weeks, the children played in groups for half an hour each day, with the goal of getting their heart rate up. As a control, one group of children engaged in quieter activities, such as painting and drawing.

The scientists decided to forgo the battery of psychological tests and simply asked parents and teachers, who were in daily contact with the children, how they perceived the results. They were asked to judge how the children's attention spans, hyperactivity and ability to focus had changed and how they got along with other kids. The children in the group that got to play didn't merely improve their ability to focus, they also experienced fewer mood swings and threw fewer temper tantrums. The biggest difference was observed at home, not in school. And while this effect was noted in all the children who were allowed to play, hyperactive or not, the biggest impact was seen in the kids who were thought to have ADHD.

This is more than simply 'burning off excess energy'

The test subjects participated in regular physical activity over several months, but positive effects on concentration were swift to manifest themselves – as little as five minutes of exercise improved concentration and lessened ADHD symptoms in the children! Maybe you think they just calmed down because they burned off some excess energy, but it wasn't quite as simple as that. The impact on their concentration was far too significant to be simply due to exhaustion.

Everyone's concentration improves

So far, the tests I've described have focused on how physical activity affects concentration in people with ADHD, and primarily in children. But what about those of us adults who do not have ADHD? Can we, too, expect to see an effect from exercise on our powers of concentration? Absolutely! Clear proof of this can be found in the outcome of a test performed on 200 pairs of 17-year-old identical twins. To measure the twins' day-to-day levels of concentration, the scientists let their parents grade them in 14 different categories, including attention, hyperactivity and impulsivity. Three years later, when the twins were 20, the parents conducted another round of grading, which showed that most of the twins had gained better concentration over that span of time. One group stood out in having markedly improved their ability to focus, and it was the twins who had been physically active in their free time. The more intense the physical activity, the more their concentration improved.

This was evident even within the pairs of twins, in cases where one twin was physically active and the other was not. In these cases, the twin who exercised had better concentration than their sibling. This indicates that the results were due to differences in lifestyle, not genes or environment. The interesting part here is that this study analysed people in their twenties who did not have ADHD. Nevertheless, it was obvious that the twins who were physically active showed better concentration and impulse control than the sedentary twins. The improvement wasn't immediate but happened over time; there was a three-year gap between the parents' ratings, after all.

WHY IS CONCENTRATION IMPROVED BY EXERCISE?

To answer this question, we must look to the past, because it's probably thanks to our ancestors and their lives on the savanna. They were physically active for reasons other than those that drive you and me to run. Today most of us run because it makes us feel good, it's healthy for us and it keeps our weight under control. Our forefathers probably didn't think about that stuff. They ran to catch food or avoid danger; in either case, they had to pay attention. There's no room for error when there's a lion behind you or you're getting ready to catch an antelope. Sharpened concentration is a survival asset in such situations. Your chances for survival increase with your brain's ability to harness additional focus. Our brains haven't evolved much since our ancestors' days on the savanna, so the same mechanism comes into play today when we exercise: the brain believes we're engaging in a potentially vital activity that requires an all-out effort, which leads us to concentrate better.

ADHD can also be an advantage

We often consider attention disorders and ADHD to be negative attributes. That's not surprising, since the symptoms must become a problem before a diagnosis can be made. However, qualities such as impulsivity and hyperactivity can also be turned to our advantage; many restless and driven people get lots of things accomplished because they don't have the patience to wait around for results. It's no accident that many successful business leaders and entrepreneurs have personality traits that call to mind ADHD.

The Ariaal tribe from the desert of northern Kenya are a good illustration of how ADHD need not be a negative trait. The tribe's members live the same way today as they did thousands of years ago, constantly moving their livestock in their search for water and food. However, in the past few decades the tribe has split into groups. One group has put down roots in one location and lives off agriculture, while the other has kept up its nomadic, hunter-gatherer lifestyle.

Scientists have examined the tribe members' genetic profile through blood tests. What interested them specifically was a gene that's essential for the function of dopamine in the brain. The gene, called DRD4, a dopamine receptor, is present in all human beings and plays an important role in concentration. It has a few variants, one of which is more common in people with ADHD. Although no single gene can cause ADHD, it is one of the most important genes involved in the condition.

The tests revealed that certain tribe members carried the DRD4 variant connected to ADHD (it's a bit clunky, but I'll call it the 'ADHD variant' for now). Other members carried the regular variant of the gene – the one not linked to ADHD. This was not unexpected. What was surprising, however, was that the nomads of the tribe who carried the ADHD variant were better nourished than those who had the regular variant. In other words, hunter-gatherers carrying the ADHD variant seemed to be better at finding food than the hunters without it. The situation was reversed when the farming tribespeople were examined. The ADHD variant carriers were *undernourished* compared to those who didn't carry it. They seemed to be worse at getting food compared to the farmers without the ADHD variant of the gene. It appears, therefore, that the ADHD variant gave an advantage to the hunters but was a drawback for the farmers; the same gene can be a strength for people living in one type of environment and a weakness for people living in another. The Ariaal tribe only split into farmers and hunter-gatherers a few decades ago, which makes the farming and hunting groups comparable to one another. One conclusion we therefore can draw is that the qualities we link with ADHD – namely impulsivity and hyperactivity – can be an advantage for hunters in an energetic environment in which they need to make quick decisions. On the other hand, the need for farmers to act fast isn't as great; in their environment, it's more important to concentrate on long-term results and work patiently, a situation in which ADHD traits might be a hindrance.

The perfect ADHD environment

That the Ariaal tribe's hunters are the ones who seem to benefit from the ADHD gene points to something interesting. There is reason to believe that even among our hunting ancestors (which is what most of our predecessors were until about 10,000 years ago, at which time agriculture was developed), there was a benefit to having this type of genetic heritage. In an environment where you hike, hunt and move from place to place depending on where the food is, restlessness and impulsivity may mean you have energy and can make snap decisions – it's almost perfect for someone who has ADHD. We've lived in that kind of environment for the vast majority of humanity's history, so from that perspective the traits we associate with ADHD today have, historically speaking, been a boon. If impulsivity and hyperactivity had caused only problems and had not provided any advantages, we would hardly encounter so many people with these characteristics nowadays; they would have been lost through natural selection.

Interestingly, the ADHD gene isn't an advantage only for hunters; it also seems to be more common in nomadic populations (I don't mean 'nomadic' in terms of changing apartments or jobs every so often; I use the term to refer to people who move around frequently). The gene seems to be associated with the desire to move around and explore new environments – a sort of 'explorer gene', if you will.

The human race originated in East Africa and gradually made its way across the planet over the past 60,000 years. Discovering new environments and seeking out unknown vistas is fundamental to our nature and has been crucial to our survival. We can suppose that this underlying drive to explore comes, to a great extent, from individuals whose personality traits we would now call ADHD.

The brain is built for movement

It isn't only among the Ariaal tribe that one lone gene can have both advantages and disadvantages depending on the environment in which it is expressed. It's the same in our society, too. Characteristics that cause trouble in one social context or type of workplace might be favourable in another. The problem is that there are no longer many situations in which ADHD qualities are an asset. Risk taking and impulsivity are rarely viewed with approval in today's world. These are behaviours we try to avoid and actively discourage in our children.

In other words, that ADHD may be an advantage if you are a hunter on the savanna is not much of a consolation. We don't hunt our food; we buy it at the supermarket. Having a gene that predisposes us to explore new environments isn't that great a deal either. We won't be rewarded for finding a new, as yet unknown fertile valley where we can settle down, because there aren't any to be found. Instead we'll be punished for not being able to sit still. The sensory hypersensitivity that is inherent to many people with ADHD means they would be able to see the tiniest of movements of prey on the savanna, which would in turn increase the likelihood of their catching it. But in school students are punished when the smallest sound distracts them from what the teacher is writing on the blackboard. Ours is a challenging time to live in for someone with ADHD; what was once considered helpful has become a bane to our modern, urban society that we try to medicate away.

From an evolutionary standpoint, looking at ADHD only as a problem is obtuse. We also know that there are other ways besides pharmaceuticals to try to solve the issues that arise from having ADHD. One way is to change your lifestyle and try to live the way we have evolved for. We can't go back to the savanna, but we can go running or hit the gym. When we do this, we'll be better equipped to handle the world that we have changed so quickly, that puts such high demands on our cognitive abilities.

Just as exercise and physical training help the ADHD sufferer to focus, they can also assist the rest of us. After all, we're all perched somewhere along the ADHD spectrum.

Maybe that's why exercise has such good results for people who have ADHD. They meet the physical challenges that we encountered so naturally in our distant past, which seem so vital to them.

Everyone's brain is built for movement, but the brain of someone with ADHD is especially attuned to it. Just as exercise helps the ADHD sufferer to focus, they can also assist the rest of us whose attention occasionally goes walkabout. After all, we're all perched somewhere along the ADHD spectrum.

TOO MUCH TIME ON THE SOFA IS DETRIMENTAL TO YOUR THINKING

You have probably seen the headlines about how spending a lot of time sitting down can increase your risk of acquiring a whole host of illnesses, but the fact is that physical inactivity has even worse consequences: it'll also make you think more slowly and poorly. American scientists followed just over 3,200 young Americans for 25 years, during which time they recorded information about how physically active they were and how much time they spent in front of the TV. In addition, different psychological tests were performed to gauge their memory, concentration skills and cognitive processing speed – i.e. how quickly they could think.

The tests clearly indicated that the test subjects who were sedentary had inferior powers of concentration and memory. They also thought more slowly. The difference was huge. The results from subjects who sat for long periods of time and those who watched TV for at least three hours a day were especially lousy.

Much of this book is about the immediate effects exercise can have on your brain, but in this case the results were very gradual, since the individuals were followed for 25 years. It shows how important physical activity is for our mental abilities, even over the long haul. Being too sedentary not only makes you unfocused, anxious and depressed, it also makes you think slower because it impairs your cognitive skills.

As you've seen in this chapter, trouble concentrating isn't caused by just one thing. The nucleus accumbens, the reward centre of the brain, is differently calibrated in different people, which affects concentration. The brain's interior noise levels can vary, and the frontal lobe might be more or less competent at quieting the noise and honing our attention.

In other words, there can be a multitude of reasons why our concentration flags, but what all of them seem to have in common is that they are affected by our level of physical activity. Fortunately, exercise efficiently tackles all these causes, and so our ability to concentrate improves.

Counteract the din with exercise

Nowadays, we produce as much digital information in two days as we did from the dawn of civilisation up to 2003. We are drowning in the data coming through our computers and smartphones in a stream that only seems to be accelerating. Meanwhile, our brain, which we expect to handle this incredible overload of information, has hardly changed at all in the last 10,000 years.

It isn't particularly surprising that our concentration sometimes wanes and that we need all the help we can get to accommodate this flow of information. The knee-jerk response to this issue cannot just consist of more diagnoses and prescription medications. We should also look at our lifestyle and see what changes we can make to improve our concentration.

Research clearly indicates that what truly puts our extra mental 'concentration gear' to work is physical exercise, not diet supplements or cognitive exercise apps. Physical activity makes us better equipped to meet a world that looks less and less like the one we have evolved for. It's in this light that you should look at training and its effects on our focus. I hope this chapter has helped you realise – whether or not you suffer from ADHD, and whether you're a kid or an adult – the good that exercise can do for your ability to focus.

THE RIGHT PRESCRIPTION FOR
IMPROVED CONCENTRATION

- Go for a run instead of taking a walk. If you move more strenuously, your brain will release more dopamine and noradrenaline. Ideally, your heart rate should reach 70–75 per cent of its maximum capacity. If you're 40, that translates to 130–140bpm. If you're 50 years old, it should be at least 125.

- Exercise in the morning. To target concentration, it's better to work out early in the day, or at least before noon, so the effects will last throughout the day. The effects will taper off after a few hours, and most of us need to focus during the day, not in the evening.

- Train for 30 minutes if you can. You should be active for at least 20 minutes, but 30 minutes is better in order to enjoy the full benefits.

- Keep up the workouts! It takes a while for exercise to affect concentration (as well as stress and general wellbeing), so don't give up! You must be patient to reap these rewards.

CHAPTER 4

THE REAL HAPPY PILL

If you are in a bad mood, go for a walk. If you are
still in a bad mood, go for another walk.

HIPPOCRATES

ONE NOVEMBER EVENING a few years ago, a colleague of mine in the hospital's emergency department where I worked asked me to see a woman in her 40s. I was given a brief history in just a few sentences: 'Previously healthy woman. Extremely fatigued for the past 24 hours. Tests and CT [computed tomography] – also CAT – scan normal. Depression?'

The woman told me she was feeling overwhelmingly tired that day. She was convinced that she had contracted some unusual disease and refused to believe that the results of all her most recent tests had come back normal. 'You must have missed something,' she said. At first she didn't understand what I was getting at when I asked how her life had been recently, but then she explained that the past year had been very demanding. She was unhappy at work because her workload had increased and her tasks had become less and less clear.

She and her husband had also bought a house, which they were in the process of renovating. That she had a lot on her plate, professionally and personally, was nothing new. This was the normal run of things for her and it had never affected her before.

This autumn, however, everything was different. She had felt increasingly exhausted. She became more and more withdrawn and wasn't bothering to keep up with friends. She used to enjoy horse riding – she had ridden competitively – and reading, but she had not been to the stables in over a year, and she could hardly remember the last time she'd cracked open a book. The urge wasn't there any more and she couldn't focus long enough to read.

That morning when she woke up she could hardly get out of bed. It was as if she had become paralysed by her lethargy, and in the end her husband brought her to the emergency room. My colleague, who first saw her, thought it might be an infection, but the blood tests were clear. Even a CT scan of the patient's brain was completely normal and didn't reveal anything suspect. The woman hesitated when my colleague suggested that she meet with a psychiatrist. After all, what she was suffering from was physical! And besides, she had never had any mental problems in her life.

This woman did in fact suffer from depression, not from some obscure malady that the physicians had missed. Once she realised this, she asked me how it could be treated. I explained that she had to slow down her commitments, maybe even take some time off work or work fewer hours, and that we could give antidepression medication a try. There was also therapy.

The woman's mother had taken antidepressants but they had had undesirable side effects, so my patient didn't want to take any pills, and she was also hesitant about therapy. Was there anything else she could do? I explained that exercise had the same effect on depression as medication, but that it would require her to take up running for least 30 minutes at a time, preferably three times per week. It would take several weeks to take effect, but once it did the outcome would be on par with that of antidepressants.

In her case, running three times a week was not a realistic goal, so we decided that she should start off with regular walks. She only managed ten-minute increments in the first few days, but gradually the walks got longer, and then faster. She was still tired when I met her at the hospital three weeks later, but she did have the energy to jog slowly for 15 minutes at a time.

As the weeks went by my patient upped her efforts. Four months after her initial visit to the ER, she was running three times a week, often close to an hour at a time. The transformation in her wellbeing was remarkable! She explained that she not only felt and slept better, she functioned better all round. Her short-term memory and concentration had also improved. Her anxiety over trivialities was gone and she didn't overreact as much to stress, whether at work or at home. She had resumed horse riding and had reconnected with her friends. In addition, she had dealt with her situation at work and had gotten clearer instructions on what was expected of her. According to her family, the difference was striking – 'Mum is back.'

What made her especially happy was that she *herself* had set these changes in motion, by getting out there on the running trail. It took a Herculean effort at the beginning, but it became easier after a while. And because this was due to her own efforts, it did wonders for her self-esteem.

Training is, in and of itself, an antidepressant. It's medication without any side effects that makes most people feel better.

ONLY SICK AND EXHAUSTED, OR DEPRESSED?

Most of us will feel down at one time or another, but you are *depressed* when you are sad week after week, when you feel despondent when thinking about the future, and when the activities you typically enjoy no longer bring you contentment. How depression expresses itself varies from person to person: some feel so exhausted that they can hardly get out of bed in the morning, while others feel so anxious that they can't sleep at night. Some lose their appetite and weight falls off them, while others become hungry and quickly put on weight. There are many types of depression, but they all have in common the enormous suffering they cause in those who are afflicted.

Today (almost) everyone knows that you can treat depression with medication. Many are also aware that exercise is good for your wellbeing, but most don't know just *how big* an impact it has, and that exercise is, in and of itself, an antidepressant. It's medication without any side effects that makes most people feel better – whether you feel just a bit blue or whether you're in the grip of a deep depression.

Training works on all types of blahs

It's challenging to properly define what constitutes depression. Many of us can feel out of sorts for a while without being depressed. There is a list of nine criteria that is used to diagnose depression: a person should have a depressed mood and increased irritability; have lost interest in things they used to find fun; feel fatigued for no apparent reason; not sleep well at night; have persistent feelings of worthlessness; have trouble concentrating; move and think slower than normal; experience recurrent thoughts of death and suicidal ideation; and have either lost or gained a lot of weight. At least five of these nine criteria should be met to diagnose depression. But what if you only check four of the criteria on the list? You may feel completely worthless and everything might seem futile. Your appe-tite might be almost gone and your sleep lousy. Does that mean you're still healthy? It's obvious you're not feeling well, but it is not, clinically speaking, depression. This example illustrates how psych-iatry is not an exact science. Basically, these are all subjective experiences; neither blood tests nor X-rays can tell if you're depressed. We use these checklists (which you can find online) in the psychiatric profession for lack of a better method; they should be considered a means of helping, not the absolute truth. Like ADHD, depression is a large grey zone.

If we prescribe an antidepressant to someone who is not suffer-ing from depression, the medication typically has no effect. However, the effects of exercise are measurable, even for people who are simply down in the dumps and not miserable enough to be diagnosed with depression. Regardless of the level of melancholy, exercise makes everyone feel better, as the negative thoughts ebb away and self-esteem gets a boost.

Many of my patients are surprised when I tell them that running has an effect that is comparable to antidepressants, since few have heard this. It's normal to wonder why so many people don't know that regular runs can be just as effective as pharmaceuticals in the fight against depression. Most seem to harbour the belief that 'if it were true, wouldn't everyone know about this already?' The reason for this widespread ignorance is very simple – it boils down to money.

PROZAC VS TRAINING

On 29 December 1987, the powerful American governmental agency the Food and Drug Administration approved the sale of the medication fluoxetine, making it the first new type of antidepressant available in the US in almost two decades. This pharmaceutical became an enormous success, even though it was introduced at a time when many still weren't convinced that depression had biological roots, or even that it originated in the brain. Fluoxetine was marketed under the name Prozac, and in short order it became not only one of the most widely sold drugs in the world but also one of the best-known brands ever.

Thousands of articles and several books, among them the cult memoir *Prozac Nation*, were written about this new pill. The rapper Jay-Z sang about it, and the character Tony Soprano from *The Sopranos* was on it.

Fluoxetine belongs to a group of pharmaceuticals called selective serotonin reuptake inhibitors (SSRIs). These increase levels of serotonin in the brain by preventing the brain cells from reabsorbing it, so that serotonin is available where it acts: *between* the cells. Within just a few years, several other drugs similar to fluoxetine were released in the marketplace and they all became hugely successful, prescribed to millions of people all over the world. But as sales skyrocketed, it became obvious that about one-third of the users saw no effects, and another third experienced only limited relief; even if they felt better, they were still depressed. Many users had side effects such as sleep disturbances, dry mouth, nausea and low libido. Some of the side effects were only temporary, but they were still unpleasant enough that some people stopped taking the medication before it had time to become effective.

Regular physical activity is as effective as pharmaceuticals in the treatment of depression.

Doctors, scientists and, not least, those who suffered from depression began to wonder whether there were other treatment options that didn't involve pharmaceuticals. It's not surprising that they chose to look at physical activity. As early as 1905, the psychiatric journal *The American Journal of Insanity* – a title that would not cut the mustard today – published a scientific article about the connection between exercise and how we feel.

At the end of 1980, scientists began to systematically compare the effect of exercise to that of medication on depression. The objective was to find out whether exercise could provide the same effects as pharmaceuticals. Naturally, this research was not funded by pharmaceutical companies – businesses that have no commercial interest in seeing whether exercise can cure depression – but by medical schools. This explains why the studies' budgets were a great deal smaller than the funding for a new pharmaceutical under development.

The breakthrough happened when American psychologist James Blumenthal gathered 156 individuals – a large group, given the field – who all suffered from depression. Blumenthal randomly assigned the subjects to three different groups. One group was given Zoloft, one of the most widely prescribed antidepressant drugs. Another group exercised for 30 minutes three times a week. The last group exercised and took the medication.

Four months later it was time to check the results. It was found that most of the test subjects felt so much better that they couldn't be considered to be depressed any more. The most important outcome was that just as many participants in the exercise group got better as those in the group that took Zoloft. In other words, regular physical activity turned out to be as effective as pharmaceuticals in the treatment of depression.

Exercise is better over the long term

Despite his study's sensational results, Blumenthal didn't rest on his laurels. He decided to carry on tracking his test subjects to see if the positive effects of exercise lasted longer than four months. That makes sense, since one emerges from depression in a fragile state, often without realising it. Many people feel great and believe that everything is back to normal, but it's easy to sink back into depression. The ice under our feet is thinner than we think.

As it happens, Blumenthal made fascinating observations at a check-in with people from the three groups six months later. During that time the participants had not been assigned to groups, but could choose for themselves what they wanted to do. Some opted for exercise, others chose therapy sessions and some took medication. Who fared better? Well, those who exercised appeared to be the least likely to relapse; fewer than one in ten, 8 per cent, became depressed again over that six-month period. On the other hand, the rate of depression in the group who took medication was more than one in three, 38 per cent. Thus exercise didn't merely provide the same shield against a new depression as medication; it offered *stronger* protection than medication.

That going for a run should be as effective as a bestselling anti-depressant pill that cost billions to develop seems almost too good to be true. Is it indeed the case that exercise produces even *better* results in overcoming depression, over the long term, than medication? Yes, this is exactly what the study showed. The results were nothing less than astonishing and were, of course, reported in the papers, but did they garner the same media exposure as the antidepressant medication? No.

Many billions of dollars have been spent on marketing anti-depressant pharmaceuticals. In contrast, how much has been spent on spreading the word that exercise has the same effect? In all likelihood, not very much. Of course, there aren't the same inherent commercial opportunities in that type of information. No one is interested in touting physical activity as widely as a pill that can generate stupendous profits and for which the marketing budget is pretty much unlimited. This is why so many people don't know about the amazing effect exercise has on depression.

More proof of the antidepressant effects of exercise

Blumenthal's results aren't unique. Recently, a group of scientists decided to compile all the papers they could find on exercise used in the treatment of depression. There were hundreds of scientific studies from the 1980s onwards, from which they selected the top 30. As many as 25 of these studies showed that exercise provides protection from depression. It's unusual to find such a large set of positive results in these situations. It looks like the research has finally caught up and shown in black and white that exercise is an excellent means of treatment for depression. And while running seems to produce the best outcome, the compendium of papers indicated that even walking is helpful in preventing depression. As little as a 20–30-minute daily walk can stave off depression and make you feel better!

The objective of all these tests was to see whether depression could be treated with physical activity, not to find the reason behind the depression. For this, we need to look at the substances in the brain that control how we feel: dopamine, serotonin and noradrenaline.

THE DRUGS DO WORK

It's important to emphasise that antidepressant medications do work. They have saved many lives and eased the suffering of millions of people. Anyone who suffers from depression should consider taking medication and should absolutely seek out professional help.

This is not about using *either* pharmaceuticals *or* training, and it is certainly not advisable for you to discontinue your medication simply because you run or cycle on a regular basis. The best effect is achieved if you use both approaches, because the combination of medication and training is especially powerful. For those who find that medication does not work for them, training might be a good alternative to drugs. Training can also be a good option for people who experience strong side effects from medication.

I want to stress that this book's purpose is not to slam medication but to show what happens in the brain when we exercise. I'm not in the least worried that there won't be enough people praising the benefits of pharmaceuticals. However, I believe that the effects achieved by exercise and training get way *too little* attention – and that's why I wrote this book.

The brain is not a chemical soup

Serotonin, noradrenaline and dopamine are molecules that transmit signals between brain cells – i.e. neurotransmitters – which is how they influence how we feel. A shortage of all three neurotransmitters has been connected to depression, and many antidepressant medications work by increasing the levels of these neurotransmitters. SSRIs, the world's most widely prescribed type of antidepressant medication, raise the level of serotonin; there are also drugs that boost levels of dopamine and noradrenaline. Serotonin, noradrenaline and dopamine do a lot more than make you feel depressed or not. They are also essential to the make-up of your personality, and for cognitive abilities such as concentration, motivation and decision-making.

Serotonin has an inhibitory effect that modulates the brain's activities. It calms overactive brain cells and suppresses activity in the entire brain so that worry and anxiety recede. Serotonin creates calm, harmony and a feeling of inner strength. A lack of serotonin can make you feel fretful and anxious.

Noradrenaline affects how alert, attentive and focused you are. Low levels of noradrenaline can make you feel tired and down, while too much of it can make you feel keyed up, hyperactive and unable to settle.

Dopamine is central to the brain's reward system and affects your motivation and drive. Food, social interaction and sex raise dopamine levels, which is why you try to get more of them. Every 'like' on social media releases a small kick of dopamine, which makes you want to check your phone again to see if you've received more. All addictive drugs, such as amphetamines, cocaine and nicotine, raise dopamine levels. Dopamine is also important for concentration and decision-making – as you've read in Chapter 3.

It would be convenient if we could draw the conclusion that anyone who is depressed lacks serotonin, noradrenaline and/or dopamine and replace what is missing with pills. Sadly it's not that simple. The image of the brain as a kind of 'chemical soup' containing the ingredients serotonin, noradrenaline and dopamine, which means we suffer from depression if we lack one or more of these ingredients, is way too simplistic. There's no way to say for sure if someone is lacking in serotonin, noradrenaline or dopamine.

One reason is because these molecules are interconnected in the brain, which means they affect not only one another but also a slew of other molecules that are pivotal to our wellbeing. This interconnectivity is so complex that we have a long way to go before we can fully grasp the extent of it. Rather, we should see the brain as an advanced network in which activities in different areas are affected, rather than a soup of poorly measured ingredients.

Regardless of this complexity, there is no doubt that serotonin, noradrenaline and dopamine are all central to our feelings. Pharmaceuticals and training can raise their levels. Physical activity can also increase serotonin, noradrenaline and dopamine, the same way anti-depressant pharmaceuticals do. The effects of exercise are typically felt *after* a workout and can last anywhere from one to a few hours. If you continue to exercise regularly, these levels will increase over time, and not just after training but over the next 24 hours.

THE BRAIN'S MIRACLE SUBSTANCE

A great mystery surrounds antidepressant medications. When they're administered to a depressed person, serotonin and dopamine levels usually rise immediately, but the person doesn't feel any better. It often takes weeks for depression to clear, and the same applies to the effects of training. Levels of dopamine and serotonin increase as soon as after the first run, but the mood lifting doesn't kick in until after several weeks of regular running.

If serotonin and dopamine play such important roles in how we feel, we should notice their effects immediately, but that's not the case. Maybe the increase in the two neurotransmitters, whether by medication or training, is just the first step towards something else that's taking place in the brain, and it's this 'something else' that makes us feel better in the end. What could it be then? In neurological research, more and more scientists are looking at what has been dubbed a miracle substance in the brain: brain-derived neurotrophic factor (BDNF).

BDNF is a protein that the brain creates in, among other places, the cerebral cortex (the brain's outer layer) and the hippocampus. We need to be careful when we call something a 'miracle', especially in medical research, but the fact is BDNF has such a positive impact on the brain that its moniker is well deserved.

When the brain cells receive BDNF, they gain protection from things that would otherwise damage or kill them. If we subject brain cells to an oxygen deficit, low blood sugar, an attack of free radicals or other toxic substances, this typically leads to cell damage or cell death, but the cells will be shielded if they get some BDNF first. If someone suffers brain damage – by having a stroke or taking a hard blow to the head, for instance – the brain seems to pump out BDNF, probably in an effort to save itself. The substance is sent out as the brain's 'rescue squad' to limit the damage, much like when our white blood cells produce antibodies to fight an infection, or when blood platelets coagulate at the site of an injury.

In addition, BDNF oversees the birth of new brain cells and helps these newly formed cells survive their vulnerable early stage. BDNF strengthens the connections between brain cells, which makes it important for learning and memory. BDNF also makes the brain more flexible and slows the ageing of the cells. The list of its benefits is so long it's almost ridiculous. BDNF is, in short, the brain's natural fertiliser. It is just as important for brain health whether we are a child, an adult or elderly.

So what does this have to do with depression? Well, BDNF is important even in cases of depression, because BDNF levels appear to be low in depressed people; this has been observed in the brains of people who have committed suicide. If a depressed person is treated with antidepressants, their level of BDNF increases. And the better you feel when recovering from depression, the more BDNF you seem to build up. But that's not all. Levels of BDNF aren't just connected to depression; they also seem to affect our personality as well. Low levels of BDNF appear to be more common in people who have a lot of the personality trait neuroticism.

Run up the fertiliser levels

And now for the big question: how can we get more of this miraculous protein? Can we swallow it in a pill? Unfortunately, no, because it would be dissolved by the acid in our stomach. And even if it were possible to protect BDNF from our stomach acid, it would not make it through the blood–brain barrier, a fancy name for the mechanism by which the brain limits what molecules it lets in. The same would happen if we injected BDNF directly into our bloodstream: the substance would not pass through the blood–brain barrier. Theoretically, we could drill a hole in the skull and inject BDNF right into it, but I don't know how many people would want to have that done – I certainly wouldn't!

However, there is a way to raise BDNF levels in a natural way, and it is – *drumroll, please!* – exercise! There is *nothing* as effective as physical activity to get the brain to make BDNF. We've seen in animal experiments that the brain immediately starts making this substance when the animal is physically active, and continues to do so for a few hours after they have stopped. A great deal of BDNF seems to be generated when the heart rate is properly elevated; it's also worth keeping up regular training, even though the brain starts producing BDNF after the initial workout, because the more active you are over time, the more BDNF your brain will produce for the same amount of exercise. Let's say you run for 30 minutes twice a week: your brain will slowly produce more and more BDNF with each run, without you having to run for longer or faster. If you quit training, the raised levels of BDNF will last for up to two weeks before they start to fall. This means that from the standpoint of BDNF alone, you don't have to be physically active every single day.

Cardiovascular exercise is responsible for increased BDNF levels; strength training doesn't appear to have the same effect. You'll need to exercise aerobically, using interval training, preferably regularly and vigorously, if you wish to generate more BDNF. Increasing the heart rate is important – if not always, then at least from time to time.

Do all roads lead to BDNF?

There are many reasons for becoming depressed or feeling low. One is going through a traumatic event, such as a divorce or a loss. Another is being subjected to long-term stress. If you walk around for extended periods with high levels of cortisol (the stress hormone) in your body, your risk of becoming depressed rises. Likewise, you can become depressed after a short burst of stress caused by an extremely intense, perhaps life-threatening event.

But often depression seems to come out of nowhere, and that's something that's being closely studied today in an effort to understand the root cause. It appears there could be other reasons for depression besides external factors; it may stem from the brain.

Somehow, depression seems to start within the body and emerges from unexpected sources. Among other things, being overweight or obese increases one's risk of suffering from depression, not only because the person feels stigmatised or stared at because of their appearance (although, of course, these can be contributing factors), but also due to something purely biological. Perhaps fat tissue releases a substance that affects the brain, which can in turn lead to depression. There are several molecules under suspicion; fatty tissue is not just a passive source of energy, it is constantly sending signals to the rest of the body to report how much energy reserves the body has. These signals are sent by a number of different molecules, of which some can affect our brain and how we feel.

We also know that people with hormonal imbalances, such as in the levels of the female hormone oestrogen, are at greater risk of depression. Further, we all have constant, low-grade inflammation in the body, which is perfectly normal. But if inflammation rises for longer periods, that can increase our likelihood of becoming depressed. Some medications inhibit inflammation – anti-inflammatory drugs – and these appear to have an antidepressant effect.

So depression seems to have many causes. Does this mean there is a common link between overweight, obesity, disturbed oestrogen levels, inflammation and the stress hormone cortisol? It looks increasingly like that could be the case, and it boils down to four letters: BDNF. In fact, it looks like all these disorders can affect BDNF.

Stress leads almost immediately to a drop in the production of BDNF. Carrying too much weight, having impaired oestrogen levels and having increased inflammation can also lead to low levels of BDNF, and that can make us feel depressed. In other words, BDNF seems to play a central, maybe even pivotal role in the development of depression, regardless of its root cause. Knowing this, we should make sure to increase our BDNF levels, which we can do by exercising. This will help no matter the cause of the depression.

Being disposed towards depression can be partly blamed on genetics – if a parent suffers from it, the chances of their offspring having it increases. But if some people carry an increased genetic risk, how does that square with BDNF? Perfectly well, it turns out!

BDNF can look a bit different from person to person, and a certain genetic variant is more common among people who suffer from depression. The fact is, BDNF is one of the few genes we could examine if we want to find out whether an individual has a genetic predisposition for depression.

THE MIRACULOUS BACKSTORY OF BDNF

The foundations for the discovery of the brain's ability to create its own fertiliser were laid down in the 1930s by Italian physician and researcher Rita Levi-Montalcini. Being Jewish, she was barred from conducting research by Italy's fascist regime, and so she lost her position as a scientist at the University of Turin. She had to flee several times during the Second World War, but she never gave up her research. Even though she had neither position nor laboratory, she continued to work in her bedroom at home, using items from her sewing kit.

Levi-Montalcini used chicken embryos as test subjects for her research into the nervous system. One day she discovered that something odd happened to the embryos in the presence of tumour cells from mice. The nerve cells in the embryos grew at record pace, including in places where they had no place growing at all, such as in blood vessels. The only reasonable explanation for this was that the tumour cells must have secreted a substance that caused rampant growth of the nerve cells. It wasn't until the 1950s that, together with German professor Viktor Hamburger, she solved the puzzle of the small protein released by tumour cells: nerve growth factor (NGF).

Levi-Montalcini soon realised that NGF didn't make all types of nerve cells grow, and she concluded that there must be several similar substances that could stimulate nerve growth. In the 1980s another such substance, which was revealed to be closely related to NGF, was discovered. It was given the name BDNF.

If quick recognition for advances in your work is what you seek, don't go into research. It wasn't until 1986 that Levi-Montalcini was awarded the Nobel Prize for Medicine in acknowledgement of her great contributions. Levi-Montalcini kept working every day into her 90s. She died in 2012 aged 103 and was at the time the oldest living Nobel Prize laureate.

New brain cells fight depression

The brain tends to shrink a little in a person who suffers from depression. Actually, this happens to everyone. From around the age of 25, the brain's size decreases by about 0.5 per cent per year, but it seems to happen more quickly in someone with depression. This is tied to, among other things, the fact that not enough new brain cells are being created. Now we know for sure that new brain cells are created even in adulthood (more about this in Chapter 5), but this regeneration is inhibited in someone who suffers from depression.

The current thinking among a growing group of neuroscientists is that depression is caused by not enough new brain cells being generated – not that the creation of new brain cells is less vigorous due to depression, but the lack of creation is in itself is the reason for the depression. Much evidence points to this hypothesis. If rats are given antidepressants, the number of brain cells being newly created in the hippocampus increases by 50 per cent. This doesn't happen overnight; it takes a few weeks for new cells to form, the same amount of time it takes for someone on antidepressant medication to begin feeling better. Is this a coincidence? If there is a correlation here – and many things indicate there might be – it means that antidepressant drugs kick-start the formation of new brain cells and clear the depression.

Medication is not the only thing that can help generate new brain cells; exercise can also jump-start the production of new cells in the hippocampus. Few things, if any, are as good at firing up the regeneration of brain cells as physical activity. And new brain cells aren't just good for those who are depressed; they also play an important role in the brain regardless of how we feel. Even those who are not depressed will benefit from new cells. So which substance is responsible for brain cell regeneration? You've guessed it: BDNF.

Your self-efficacy can cure you

Several things happen in the brain when we become depressed: levels of dopamine, serotonin, noradrenaline and BDNF fall, and fewer new brain cells are created. We don't yet know which of these factors is the most relevant (it's more than likely they're all linked), but we do know that physical exercise helps.

Feeling down or being depressed is kind of like being at a mental standstill. Moving your body is diametrically opposed to this.

Aside from having a biological impact on newly created brain cells and on molecules such as dopamine and BDNF, there are other reasons why exercise is good for us, and why it's a good treatment for depression. One of them, as with my female patient in the ER, is that you can get a handle on the situation yourself. You're actively doing something to get well – in her case, she started to run. In psychological research the term 'self-efficacy' is often used, which basically means 'belief in one's own ability to complete a task or reach a goal'. It may sound a bit hollow, but it is in fact an established psychological concept. When you increase self-efficacy, you feel pleased with yourself. You can increase your self-efficacy through regular exercise, and that goes for kids as well.

Feeling down or being depressed is kind of like being at a mental standstill, where you are unable to make any progress in life. Everything slows down and the brain receives fewer impressions. Moving your body is diametrically opposed to this. Depression also often means you withdraw and stop socialising with people, and you no longer engage in what you used to enjoy. Consequently the brain gets less stimulation and you feel even worse; it becomes a vicious circle. John Ratey, an American psychiatrist at Harvard University, describes depression as a loss of contact with the sufferer's human connections, as well as the person's brain cells. Engaging in physical activity is one way to break this vicious cycle. You get out, meet people and become less solitary; at the same time, your brain cells break out of their isolation.

These sorts of behavioural changes are often more difficult to measure than, say, levels of dopamine and BDNF, for which you can obtain a number. But just because terms such as 'self-efficacy' and 'behaviour modification' don't sound as verifiable as 'increased levels of dopamine', this doesn't mean they're not important.

A more positive personality

The woman you read about in the beginning of this chapter is just one of many people who felt much better after starting regular work-outs. In her case, as well as several others, it seemed like her entire personality changed for the better. At first I thought this was just a coincidence. Surely exercise can't transform your *personality*? But as a matter of fact, research shows that people who train regularly don't just become happier, they also seem to experience small changes in fundamental personality traits.

Research in Finland, Japan and South Africa has shown that those who exercise regularly tend to be less cynical and less neurotic. In addition, they feel greater rapport with people in their environment. The exact same pattern was observed in Holland when researchers examined close to 20,000 pairs of twins. Those who exercised twice a week were more socially open and less neurotic.

The answer to which comes first – the exercise or the reduced neuroticism – is, of course, not obvious. Exercise could make a person less cynical and less neurotic, but it might also indicate that people who are cynical and neurotic don't exercise as much. So how can one know what is the chicken and what is the egg? It seems that exercise actually affects personality (rather than vice versa), and that is because we're gradually beginning to understand the role of mol-ecules in certain personality traits.

Serotonin and dopamine aren't just important for how you feel – the variations in people's levels of these molecules probably contribute to differences in personality. Dopamine, for example, has been linked to curiosity and a willingness to try new experiences, while serotonin is linked to compromise and also to how neurotic a person is.

Boiling personality down to molecules is not easy. The biology determining your personality is tremendously complex, and neurotransmitters such as dopamine and serotonin can't begin to explain your entire personality. That being said, personality *is* in the end just biology: it is in the brain that your personality is located. The fact that dopamine and serotonin levels are influenced, over the short and long term, by exercise means that it is not at all unreasonable to suppose that exercise can affect personality.

Exercise becomes a drug

One of the effects of exercise on how we feel is more extreme than others. It's a fact that we can feel completely high from moving our bodies, in which case exercise becomes a sort of endogenous drug (i.e. a drug that originates within our bodies). I am talking about what is commonly known as the 'runner's high', which you might have experienced yourself. You should not chase the runner's high if you're suffering from depression, but it still deserves a mention in this book. The story of what it is and what causes it is nothing short of thrilling.

The hunt for mystical morphine

Humans have known for over 2,000 years that opium can blot out pain and cause euphoria. Dried sap from the opium poppy, from which opium is made, was used as a medicine and a popular drug during the Roman Empire. At the start of the nineteenth century, German scientists managed to isolate morphine, the active ingredient in opium, and began using it in healthcare, most notably as a painkiller for wounded soldiers. It proved to be amazingly effective. Even when soldiers had lost arms or legs, small doses in tenth-of-a-gram increments could knock out their pain. It seemed incredible that such a low dose could have so deep an impact, especially when compared to alcohol, which can achieve a similar effect but only in doses hundreds of times larger.

At the beginning of the 1970s it was discovered that there is a type of receptor on the surface of brain cells that morphine binds to, which explains why the drug is so powerful. This raised the question of why these receptors even exist. Does nature want us to turn into morphine addicts? That didn't seem likely; a more plausible reason was that the brain could produce its own morphine-like substance, and that the receptors were meant for this self-made and as yet unknown substance.

Scientists all over the world raced to try to identify the brain's morphine, and those efforts quickly produced results. In 1974 it was discovered that pigs' brains released a mysterious substance with a similar structure to morphine. That same year, the American psychiatrist Solomon H. Snyder made the same discovery when he examined calves' brains. The mysterious substance found in the pigs and the calves, which turned out to be several closely related substances, was the sought-after 'self-morphine'.

This substance, which exists even in humans, acquired the name 'endogenous morphine', meaning 'morphine originating from the body'. It has since become known by a shorter name: endorphins.

Endorphins are, like morphine, incredibly effective at suppressing pain. And just like morphine, they can produce feelings of euphoria. But why would the brain reward itself with a dose of morphine? Why does this mechanism exist and when does the brain reward itself? The question was raised as to whether there is a natural circumstance in which human beings experience pain relief and euphoria simultaneously, without the help of medication or drugs.

American long-distance runner James Fixx explains a state such as this in his bestseller, *The Complete Book of Running*. Sometimes when Fixx was running long distances, he experienced a feeling of euphoria and pain relief that he called 'runner's high'. He was far from alone in experiencing this – reports soon came in from other athletes who participated in different types of aerobic training. Swimmers, cyclists and rowers had all felt the same sensation but simply called it by different names. Rowers called it, appropriately enough, 'rower's high'.

Run yourself high!

James Fixx's book came out during the running craze of the 1970s; 'runner's high' soon became a buzzword, and it was widely accepted that the newly discovered endorphins were at the crux of this effect. Today most runners know about runner's high, but far from all have experienced it.

The effect is so much stronger than simply feeling a bit more alert – runner's high is the most extreme impact training can have on our mood. I myself have felt it twice, and it's impossible to explain other than to say it's pure magic! It's not the same calm you feel at the end of a workout. No, it's more akin to euphoria, when all pain disappears, all impressions become more intense and you feel like you could run forever and ever, as fast as the wind. The feeling is so intense that you will most definitely remember it if you ever experience it. If you're unsure whether you've felt runner's high, it's likely you haven't.

It seems logical that endorphins are behind this feeling, because it is so reminiscent of the effect of morphine. However, the source of runner's high is still being debated, and some scientists believe there's more to this happy state than just endorphins. To shed some light on the issue, a few scientists in Munich, Germany, decided to examine the brains of runners in their local runners' club. They measured the level of endorphins with a positron emission tomography (PET) scan before and two hours after a high-speed run. The results were unambiguous: all the runners had lots of endorphins after the run, especially in their prefrontal cortex and limbic systems, two areas of the brain that are especially important for feelings. When the runners rated their levels of euphoria, it was obvious that the more euphoria they reported feeling, the more endorphins were present in their brain.

This is where the debate around what causes runner's high could have ended, but there are a few arguments against the notion that endorphins are the sole reason for this feeling. First, endorphin molecules are large, which means it difficult for them to break the blood–brain barrier. Second, when long-distance runners were given a substance to block morphine, and thus by extension endorphins, runners could still feel the runner's high.

Are highs only caused by endorphins?

Another possibility is that runner's high is caused by endocannabinoids. Like endorphins, they are a type of painkilling substance produced by the body, but they are smaller than endorphins and can therefore make their way into the brain more easily. Like endorphins, there are specific receptors for endocannabinoids on the brain cells that addictive drugs can bind to (endocannabinoids use the same receptors in the brain as the active ingredient in hashish and marijuana).

The suggestion that endocannabinoids might have something to do with runner's high was bolstered when French scientists genetically modified mice so that they lacked endocannabinoid receptors, and the rodents' desire to move subsequently changed. Normally for mice to run of their own accord it's enough that they have a cage with a wheel. However, the genetically modified mice didn't care to move at all and only ran half as much as mice typically do. The extent to which a mouse can experience euphoria and runner's high is difficult to assess, but it has been seen that levels of endocannabinoids increase in humans after they run. Walking is not enough for this – a person must run for at least 45–60 minutes. This dovetails with what's required to reach a runner's high – by definition it cannot be achieved by walking.

Some scientists believe that, aside from endorphins and endocannabinoids, runner's high comes from increased levels of dopamine and serotonin. Others believe it's linked to body temperature and that we become euphoric as we heat up. The most plausible explanation is that runner's high doesn't rely on one single factor but rather several of them, and that endorphins and endocannabinoids both contribute to it. Whatever the biological source may be, it is mostly only of interest to scientists. For runners, cyclists and tennis players – or whoever else experiences a high from being physically active – it's enough to know *that* runner's high happens, not *why* it happens.

Our heritage from the savanna

Becoming euphoric from running is probably a leftover effect from our ancestors' lives on the savanna. No doubt some of them had to run long distances while hunting – a method that Aboriginal Australians and Kalahari Desert bushmen still use. When our ancestors stalked prey for several miles to tire it out, it was important not to give up the chase, and so endorphins came in handy. If you twisted your ankle or your muscles ached, endorphins blotted out the pain, and when the going got tough that feeling of euphoria made it easier to keep going. This increased the likelihood of a kill, which is probably why we still experience runner's high today.

That runner's high may be a natural way to get us to keep running and catch our food is not just speculation. For instance, it has been shown that if we decrease our level of body fat, our levels of leptin – a hormone released by fat – also decrease, which sounds the alarm that energy levels are dropping and need to be topped up. Our body doesn't want us to be skinny – quite the opposite, in fact. It wants us to carry around a substantial reserve of energy. If this hypothesis is correct – that we need a shot of pleasure to keep up the strength to search for food – then our body is telling us, via runner's high: 'Your stores of energy will soon be depleted. Don't give up, keep moving and find more food!' To help us along, it makes us feel euphoric.

How do you achieve runner's high?

We know that you must run for at least 45 minutes, and the more you run, the greater the chance of feeling runner's high. The brain appears to give itself ever-increasing doses of endorphins the more you train. Consequently the likelihood of feeling runner's high increases over time, so don't give up! However, there are no guarantees; not everyone will get to feel it.

It has been shown that your pain threshold increases when you've been running for a while – the same as with morphine. By jabbing people with a needle or pinching them to test their tolerance to pain, we've noticed that it takes more for someone to feel pain during running than at rest. This supports the idea that endorphins not only make us feel euphoric but also provide pain relief. And there is no doubt that the pain relief can be powerful: it has been calculated that the endorphins felt during high-speed running are equal to a 10ml shot of morphine, a commonly administered dose for an arm or leg fracture. That's why we sometimes see runners keep running even when they have stress fractures (fractures caused by long-term overuse and repetitive motion). They don't feel the pain so long as they run, and it flares up the moment they stop and the effect of the endorphins wears off. While runner's high is exercise's most extreme effect on the brain, your wellbeing will improve through exercise even if you don't feel a dramatic rush of endorphins. Anyone who exercises is rewarded with endorphins and endocannabinoids, even if they don't reach the runner's high.

THE RIGHT PRESCRIPTION TO FEEL BETTER OVERALL

Do you feel tired and down in the dumps? Then get out and run! Running, or participating in an activity that raises your heart rate, can work wonders, so long as you do it often and for extended periods. You should keep the following guidelines in mind:

- Exercise is hard if you feel down so start slowly. Start by just walking 30–40 minutes three times a week, then slowly build on this until you can run for the same length of time. The intensity should be at least 70 per cent of your VO_2 max, which means that you break a sweat and can't say long sentences without catching your breath. This is the point at which exercise becomes a powerful antidepressant.
- Cycling or any other types of cardiovascular training are good substitutes for running. It's the intensity and length of time that count, not what you do or where you do it.
- Keep this up for at least three weeks! It's true that many people feel better after exercising just once, but to feel better during the whole day and not just after a workout, you need to train regularly over several weeks. Don't expect too many results in the first few weeks.

If you suffer from depression

Exercise is as effective as antidepressant medication for mild or non-clinical depressive conditions, but to get an effect comparable to medication you must run (or partake in an equivalent type of exercise) three times a week for 45 minutes at a time. It takes about six weeks to notice some changes, so don't give up!

Medication works best for severe depression and suicidal thinking. If you're suffering from these conditions, it's not realistic to expect yourself to start exercising, since it might take all your strength just to get out of bed. *Always* speak to your physician and *never* quit your medication on your own!

Again, it's not a question of either/or here. Training is good. Medication is good. The ideal is a combination of both. Regular exercise and physical activity could also help prevent future depressive episodes. You also become more resilient to stress, which is the most common cause of depression. Everything is connected!

CHAPTER 5

JOG YOUR MEMORY

Take care of all your memories. For you cannot relive them.

BOB DYLAN

IN THE MID-1990S, a group of scientists decided to see which part of the brain is most affected by exercise. They already had a theory before the study began: the cerebral cortex and the cerebellum (situated in the back of your head where the spinal cord meets the brain) are both important for the coordination of physical movement, so it seemed natural that these areas would be the most affected by physical activity, just as running has more influence on cardiovascular fitness than on muscular strength.

The starting point was to see which part of the brain creates the most BDNF (the brain's own miracle medication, described in the previous chapter) in mice that run on a wheel in their cage. The strange thing was that when the mice's brains were examined, it was revealed that neither the cortex nor the cerebellum produced the most BDNF, but the hippocampus – the brain's memory centre. This discovery became one of the most important clues as to why exercise has such a huge effect on memory. Over the past decade, research on animals and humans has proved that our memory is strengthened by physical activity. In fact, nothing seems to be more important for memory than physical activity.

STOP YOUR BRAIN FROM SHRINKING

The brain shrinks throughout life, and unfortunately this process begins much earlier than most of us would like. The brain is at its largest when we're about 25 years old, after which it gets a little smaller every passing year. Certainly, new brain cells are created throughout our lifetime, but cells die more quickly than new ones are generated. The net effect is that we lose approximately 100,000 brain cells every 24 hours. This goes on 24/7, year round. Even though there are plenty of cells to begin with – the brain contains about 86 billion cells – the loss will become noticeable over time. Over one year, the brain's volume will decrease by about 0.5 per cent.

The memory centre, the hippocampus – as big as a thumb and shaped like a seahorse – is one of the areas of the brain that shrinks as we age. Its size decreases by about 1 per cent each year. We have two hippocampi, one in each hemisphere of the brain, and they are located deep inside each temporal lobe. A slowly but steadily shrinking hippocampus is probably one reason why our memory gets worse as the years go by.

For a long time, we thought that shrinkage of the hippocampus could only be adversely impacted. You could *speed it up*, and thus accelerate the brain's ageing, by consuming large quantities of alcohol or using drugs, but slowing down or reversing the shrinkage was considered impossible. It is against this backdrop that we will now see some of the most convincing evidence for the amazing effects exercise and physical training have not only on memory but on the brain as a whole. American scientists used MRI scans to examine the brains of 120 individuals; they measured their hippocampi at two different times, with a year in between. The test subjects were randomly assigned to two groups that performed two different types of activities. One group did endurance training, while the other engaged in mellower exercises like stretching that did not raise their heart rate.

One year later, the members of the group who did endurance training had become fitter, in contrast to the group that had performed the gentler exercises. Nothing surprising so far, but what had happened to their hippocampi? The hippocampi in people who had done the gentle exercises had shrunk by 1.4 per cent, which was no surprise either, since the hippocampus does shrink by about 1 per cent each year.

What was very suprising was that the hippocampi hadn't shrunk at all in the members of the group who had done endurance training; in fact, they had *grown* and become larger by 2 per cent. Instead of ageing by a year, the hippocampi had 'rejuvenated' themselves and, in terms of size, become two years younger! And that's not all: the fitter the test subjects had become, the larger their hippocampi had grown. Among those who had seen the greatest improvement in their fitness, their hippocampi had grown by more than 2 per cent.

Of course, this raises the very important question of how this happened. One not unreasonable hypothesis is that the brain's fertiliser, BDNF (which increases as we become more physically active), played a role. In the previous chapter, we learned that BDNF can strengthen the bond between brain cells and can thereby influence how well we remember things. When the scientists examined the levels of BDNF in the test you just read about, they noticed that the more the levels had risen, the more the hippocampus had grown.

You can stop, and may even reverse, your brain's ageing by power-walking or running a few times a week!

What miraculous training programme could revitalise and promote regrowth of such an important part of the brain in a single year? Did the test subjects pedal away on stationary bikes like bats out of hell, or run at draconian intervals? Not at all. They neither cycled nor ran. The only exercise they engaged in was a 40-minute power-walk three times a week. This means that you can stop, and may even reverse, your brain's ageing, and strengthen your memory, by power-walking or running a few times a week!

However, it's important to be cautious when drawing conclusions from these kinds of tests. Experiments are one thing, reality is another. If the hippocampus can be protected from ageing, or even be 'rejuvenated' and grow bigger, what does that mean for us in our lives? Do we truly see improvement in our memory just by being physically active? The short answer is yes, absolutely!

The walking group in the experiment had not only grown their hippocampi, their memory had also improved, especially their spatial memory (their ability to remember a three-dimensional space). This effect was dose dependent, meaning the participants who had increased the size of their hippocampus the most had the most improved memory. Interestingly, these individuals had also increased their cardiovascular fitness the most.

A large number of tests point clearly in the same direction: both short- and long-term memory are improved through exercise, and the gradual breakdown of the hippocampus that comes with ageing can be slowed down and even reversed.

Genetic rejuvenation of the brain

As if it weren't enough that exercise protects the hippocampus from age-related shrinkage, it appears that it also offers protection against genetic ageing. Just like other cells in the brain and body, the hippocampus contains our genetic material. All of our genes can be found in every brain cell. Normally genes don't change during our lifetime, but our *use* of them changes, which can cause the body's organs, including the brain, to age.

If we examine hippocampus brain cells in mice at different ages, we'll find that in a number of genes the activity changes as the animals age. These changes follow the animals' ageing. Among other things, these genes control the growth of brain cells and their ability to create connections to each other. As the mice age, these genes become less active, and this gradual genetic change doesn't just make the hippocampus age, it makes the entire brain grow older.

However, not even cells ageing at the *genetic* level means we're doomed and have no recourse. When the test animals ran on a treadmill, something happened that can only be described as amazing. Many of the genes that were adversely affected by ageing were also influenced by exercise, but in a positive way. Through mechanisms that are not yet fully understood, the hippocampus cells appeared to become *genetically* younger after the test animals ran.

These effects were powerful but not instantaneous. The mice ran daily for eight weeks, which for us would be the equivalent of exercising regularly for several years, meaning that the occasional jog is not enough. But intriguingly, it seems that those who remain physically active regularly over a long period of time not only grow a larger hippocampus, they are also rewarded with revitalised hippocampus cells.

PRACTICAL MEMORY TRAINING

How do we go about strengthening memory through physical activity? Do we need to keep at it for several months or can we notice effects right away? Does it work best *before* learning something or is it better to exercise *after* learning?

You don't have to work out for very long in the beginning to notice an effect. It has been shown that three months of regular endurance training can lead to significant improvement in the ability to recall words. And it's worth putting in the effort, because *how* much better your memory gets – i.e. the number of words you can remember – is connected to how much fitter you become. In the test that showed that a year of regular fast walks cause the hippocampus to grow by 2 per cent, those who improved their fitness the most also saw the most benefit to their memory. This link is especially interesting considering that the hippocampus grows larger as we get fitter.

Do you think three months is a long time? Don't worry, you'll notice results quicker than that. In one study, healthy individuals who cycled regularly on stationary bikes were compared to a group of similar-aged folk who did not cycle. Before the test began, the participants in both the group that was about to cycle and the one that wasn't had comparable results on several different memory tests. However, the cyclists soon pulled ahead in both fitness and memory. Six weeks in, it was obvious that the group that cycled were better at the memory tests, and the differences increased the longer the study lasted. The cyclists' memory kept improving, while the non-cyclists stayed in one spot, both in terms of fitness and memory.

When the cyclists' brains were studied via MRI, the scans revealed that improved memory went hand in hand with increased blood flow to the hippocampus. This increased blood flow would certainly explain why the hippocampus worked better. Interestingly, it looks like the blood flow increased first, then memory improved.

If you'd like to boost your memory, you will need to move and learn at the same time.

An instant memory boost

Are you as impatient as I am and feel that six weeks is way too long to wait for progress? The fact is, exercise improves memory immediately! It has been observed that those who did best on the test were those who exercised right *before* the test. Moderately fit people who exercise right before a memory test typically do better than fit people who haven't trained beforehand, so it appears exercise has an immediate effect on memory.

But if you'd like to boost your memory to the max, you will need to move and learn at the same time – studying while walking on a treadmill, for instance. This is good to keep in mind even if it may not always be practically possible.

We don't know why individuals who learn things during or soon after they exercise remember them better. What probably happens is that the blood flow in the brain increases when you move, the same way blood circulation increases in the muscles. This blood flow boost is instantaneous, and when the brain gets more blood, memory works better.

Don't work out to the point of failure

Boosting your memory through exercise doesn't just give a marginal effect that can only be measured in scientific experiments; on the contrary, you will be able to notice these effects. In tests that measure word recall, it has been shown that you can learn up to 20 per cent more words if you're physically active before or while you learn the words, compared to when you are at rest. Those of you who are studying for an exam or need to learn material for work should think twice before deciding you don't have time for a walk. That walk is probably time well spent.

From a memory standpoint, walking or light jogging is enough to achieve the best effect. However, if you work out to the point of failure and end up exhausted, you run the risk of remembering slightly *less*. The reason is that when you exercise intensely, your muscles require so much blood that the blood flow to the brain decreases slightly, which may be why your cognitive functions, memory included, don't work as well during and just after strenuous exercise. Besides, if you exercise intensely, the brain seems to focus on your movement and not on what you're trying to learn. If you run fast while listening to something you need to remember, your brain is going to focus on running, not what you're listening to.

Can running make me a better piano player?

Memory is not all about learning words, reading texts or remembering what we did last week. We also have motor memory for movements, like when we learn to hit a forehand in tennis or play a piano piece. The basis for all learning is that new connections are created between brain cells, which might make you wonder whether the conditions for learning a motor skill improve if you exercise. Naturally your forehand will get better if you practise only that movement. But does this mean the conditions for learning the forehand improve if you run first? Or that cycling can improve your ability to play the piano?

To gauge how physical activity influences motor memory, subjects were asked to play a simple computer game using a joystick to follow a point moving across a screen. The game might seem simplistic, but it activates many areas of the brain and is occasionally used to measure motor ability.

For this test, subjects were first required to run or cycle and then they proceeded to the computer game. After a while they were asked to play the game again to see whether they had improved. Just as your forehand improves with practice, you also naturally improve at playing a computer game after some practice. But here's what is worthy of note: when tested, those who had been physically active prior to playing the game were better at it! Moreover, this increased aptitude was still recorded 24 hours after the individual first tried the game, and again one week after learning the game. To be clear: the only difference was that some of the test subjects exercised before they tried it; there were no variations in the time they spent practising the game. Nonetheless, those who exercised did better. Some aspect of movement in and of itself made them learn the game better without having to spend more time practising.

How then can physical activity make us perform better at a motor activity? We can only speculate, but in the minutes to hours following the acquisition of a new skill there is 'memory consolidation'. This means the memory – whether it's German vocabulary, a piano piece or a computer game – is transferred from short- to long-term memory. Let's say you play a simple tune on the piano a few times, then you rest for one minute and play the tune again. You'll probably remember it quite well as it's sitting in your short-term memory. But how well will you remember that tune tomorrow? That depends on how strongly the memory has been imprinted, or consolidated, as a long-term memory.

MENTAL PATHS

Basically, our memories are clusters of brain cells connected to one another. When we experience something new – i.e. create a new memory – new connections called 'synapses' are created. 'Connection' doesn't mean the cells physically touch each other; rather end terminals on the cells send a chemical message between them. The Nobel Prize winner Santiago Ramón y Cajal described it poetically as brain cells holding hands, even though the cells don't actually touch.

How hard cells hold on to one another depends on how many times they make contact. If you learn a new phone number, a new contact will be created. Each time you dial that number the contact will strengthen – the cells will hold on tighter to each other – and you'll remember the number much better each time you dial it. Perhaps you remember that 'neurons that fire together, wire together'? On the other hand, if you only use the phone number once, you will forget it. The connection will weaken if it isn't reinforced and the brain cells will lose their connection.

Similarly, we can look at memories as mental paths that are created between the brain's cells. Well-trodden paths stay put and so that memory remains. Paths that are walked on only a few times will grow over and disappear.

Some things create a well-worn path right away that embeds a memory for life. A unique or unusually intense experience can leave a lifelong mental imprint even if the path was only 'walked on' once. This applies especially to emotionally charged events that have negative connotations, such as threats or danger. These types of memories are very important from a survival standpoint and they consequently have priority in the memory bank.

Evolutionarily speaking, it's critical to remember what is dangerous so you can avoid it in the future. This means that if you witness something horrible or experience a life-threatening situation, you will most likely remember the event in detail for the rest of your life. Other things that are not as unique or charged, like tying your shoelaces, won't leave a path. The cells hold on to each other for a short while and then they let go. You'll quickly forget you did it.

Bearing this in mind, you can see how physical activity can contribute to mental paths becoming well worn and to cells 'holding on hard to each other'. As you'll recall from the beginning of this chapter, exercise leads to the brain cells in the hippocampus pumping out more of the substance BDNF. BDNF strengthens the connections between brain cells so they 'hold hands even harder', which, to continue the analogy, means the mental path becomes well worn more quickly. The memory becomes stronger and, consequently, we remember what we're doing. We remember better and we learn better.

Physical activity increases levels of BDNF, which in turn reinforces the connections between brain cells, making this probably one of the most important reasons why exercise is so beneficial for memory.

The hippocampus is important for how memories get transferred from short- to long-term memory. As we've seen, exercise makes the hippocampus cells pump out BDNF, which reinforces the connections between brain cells. If we engage in physical activity before learning, BDNF will be released while the memory moves from short to long term. Thus, the conditions for that memory to go into long-term storage will probably improve because the transmission from short- to long-term status doesn't happen within minutes of learning something but more like *24 hours* afterwards. This corresponds quite closely to what the computer game test revealed: that exercise starts having an effect one day after learning.

This means you'll probably become a better piano player if you're physically active before you practise your piano scales! And you'll probably increase your chances of learning that golf swing if you go for a run or a bike ride before heading out on the golf course. Through exercise, you can strengthen your memory during that crucial phase when the piano piece or the golf swing – or whatever skill it is you wish to learn – is being saved to long-term memory. The brain cells' ability to create strong and lasting connections between one another increases, and this seems to apply whether you want to acquire a language or a motor skill.

A long walk or a 30-minute run is plenty for the brain – it's probably better than running for several hours.

Does too much training impair memory?

From the brain's perspective, it's debatable whether more exercise is always better, or if you can have too much of a good thing. Is a gruelling race such as the Ironman, during which participants remain active for 10–12 continuous hours, good for memory and the brain? We don't know for sure yet, but there are reasons to suspect that such a big effort is more damaging than beneficial to the brain and the memory – at least in the short term.

By selecting from a large pool of mice, American scientists were able to breed specimens that were obsessed with running. Those that ran the most could mate, and the offspring that moved the most were in turn allowed to mate. The scientists continued in this manner until they had produced mice that would, of their own free will, run almost three times as much as regular mice. In fact, these 'ultrarunner' mice ran the equivalent of many miles a day for a human being.

The mice's memory was tested by letting them try out a new maze. Normally, mice that have been running are faster at finding their way around a new space, because training improves memory. However, the ultrarunner mice took much longer than normal to learn the new maze. Their memory was worse and they had high levels of the stress hormone cortisol in their blood. Cortisol is central to the body's stress response and its level typically drops after we've been physically active. But these mice ran regularly, so they should have had less stress and lower cortisol levels. Instead, these ultrarunners seemed to be chronically stressed out.

We don't yet know for certain whether this carries over to humans, but it looks like there is a degree to which exercise can become too much for the brain to handle. At this point the stress response no longer decreases but *increases* and memory becomes poorer. We don't know exactly where that stress cut-off is, but it probably varies from person to person. However, one conclusion that could possibly be drawn is that anyone who participates in ultramarathons or similar events should not do so with the intention of strengthening their brain and improving their memory, because they may in fact suffer the opposite outcome. A long walk or a 30-minute run is plenty for the brain – it's probably much better than running for several hours.

YOUR BRAIN CAN CREATE NEW CELLS

In the early 1990s, most scientists agreed that the adult brain could not generate any new cells. If we cut ourselves, the cut heals over and new skin cells are produced. Likewise, new hair cells and blood cells form. Most of the body's organs are capable of regenerating cells, but almost no researchers thought this to be true of the brain; the explanation was that the brain, which is comprised of 86 billion cells, is so incredibly complex that newly generated brain cells in an adult brain could not fit with the cells originating from birth. It seemed as improbable as thinking you could dismantle a computer, randomly plug in a few circuit boards and hope the computer would run better. This belief is why many of us were taught in school that the brain we have at 20 years old is the one we must make do with for the rest of our lives. I remember also being told in school that 'if you take a swig of alcohol, you'll lose 50,000 brain cells that you'll never see again'.

It doesn't hurt to question established 'truths' from time to time, and in the mid-1990s a group of scientists in California decided to take a good look at the question of whether the adult brain can produce new cells. They didn't start off by examining human brains but those of mice. The first question they wanted to clear up was whether anything would happen in their brains if the animals were removed from their boring, sterile cages and got more stimulation in an 'enriched environment'. The mice lived for one month in a cage with plenty of tunnels to hide in, wheels to run on and toys to play with. They also had the company of more mice. This was indisputably a far more stimulating environment than the sterile cages the mice were used to. The scientists knew that a change of environment with new experiences could create new connections between the mice's brain cells, because connections are created when we learn something new. But could it affect the animals' brains in other ways? Indeed it did!

The new, stimulating environment had a huge effect on the brain: it created lots of new cells. Part of the mice's hippocampi grew and the repercussions were dramatic. The number of cells increased by 15 per cent in a few short weeks, which was sensational.

This couldn't be explained by the mice's young age, because the same thing occurred when the scientists performed an identical experiment on older mice. The mice's brains didn't just generate new cells, the mice seemed to function better cognitively. When the mice's memory was tested by lowering them into a pool in which they had to find a hidden platform, the mice that had been in the enriched environment located the platform faster. They also had a better memory than the mice that had been in a sterile cage.

What exactly caused this effect?

This discovery has stunning implications. Could it also apply to people put in more stimulating environments? Does this mean that a change of environment and new experiences such as travel, a career change or a new social circle could lead the brain to create new cells? Could such experiences improve our memory and perhaps even make us smarter?

But before we move on, let's pause and ask: what was it in the mice's environment that made their brains create more cells? Was it the toys and the tunnels where they could hide, or was it that there were many other mice around? Or could it have had something to do with the wheel they were running on?

I would have guessed that it was a combination of all these factors. But it turns out, I would have been wrong. When the mice *only* ran on the wheel and didn't have access to any other stimulus in their crate, the impact on their brain was widespread. It appears that physical activity – running on the wheel – was the principal factor in the creation of new brain cells. Other stimuli, from toys to tunnels, appeared to have little or no effect.

Finding out that regular running produces so many new brain cells had significant repercussions for several of the scientists. One of them, geneticist Fred 'Rusty' Gage, explained how his colleagues turned their lifestyles around completely and began running as soon as they saw the new cells in the mice's brains. They reasoned that if it works in mice, it probably works in humans, too.

But were Gage and his colleagues correct in inferring that the adult brain can generate new brain cells? This is a difficult question to answer, because it would require studying the brain under a microscope; a CT scan or MRI cannot provide any clues. In fact, what is needed is an autopsy of a human brain. But even if someone agreed to donate their brain in the name of research after their death, there would still be a problem: how do you figure out if the brain cells are new? It's extremely challenging to tell the difference between old and new brain cells.

DO WE ALWAYS REMEMBER PAIN ACCURATELY?

Many times I've heard the lament 'never again' from marathon runners who have just crossed the finish line. And yet, a few months later, there they are, signing up for another race. How is it that you can go through a race that you consider intolerably difficult and still choose to line up at the starting blocks year after year? A possible explanation is that runners forget how exhausting the event was.

Selective forgetfulness is not some pseudo-psychological term but a medical reality that happens at times such as after childbirth. When a comparison was made between how women experienced labour pains and the pain they felt after gynaecological surgery, it showed that those who had given birth and those who had had surgery rated the pain at about the same intensity. The pain of childbirth appears to be comparable to that of surgery.

But when you ask the women who gave birth to remember the event and the pain a few months later, it turns out that they no longer remember how traumatic it was. However, those who had undergone surgery remembered the pain as vividly as the day it was performed. Many women do indeed 'forget' just how painful it is to give birth. It's one thing to remember that it is painful and another to remember the *intensity* of that pain. From a biological perspective this isn't so strange, because if there's one thing that's vital for our species, it's procreation.

THE MIND-BODY METHOD

That's why it makes sense for there to be a natural mechanism for 'forgetting' labour pain, or at least for not remembering the pain in so much detail that you would not want to give birth again.

The same thing appears to happen with hard physical exertion. When marathon runners who crossed the finish line graded the pain they felt throughout the race on a 10-point scale, the average answer was 5.5. But when they thought back to the race and regraded their pain 3–6 months later, their answer went down to 3.0. They seemed to have forgotten just how painful it was!

If we think about it, even this 'selective memory' is reasonable, from a biological perspective. If we remember how hard it was to follow our kill over long distances, it may discourage us and make us give up on hunting. However, if we forget how tiring it was, we'll be eager to go hunting again, which increases our chances of getting food and, in the long run, of surviving. This is a likely explanation for our ability to selectively 'forget' the pain inherent in physical activities.

Even adults generate new brain cells

The solution came when Swedish neuroscientist Peter Eriksson had a brilliant idea. Oncologists use a substance called bromodeoxyuridine (BrdU) to detect whether cancer cells divide and thereby determine if the cancer is growing. BrdU can tag new cells – and not just cancer cells but other types of cells as well. Eriksson realised that if there were new brain cells in the brain samples of dead cancer patients, BrdU would be able to tag them, too, making it possible to pick them out.

No sooner was it said than it was done, and the researchers obtained permission to examine the brains of five deceased patients to look for new cells. Their brains offered a unique insight into the question of whether the brain regenerates throughout life – one of neuroscience's biggest conundrums. It was hoped that, upon examination, the samples would reveal brain cells marked with BrdU in at least one of the donors. In fact, they found cells in all five, and in exactly the same area of the brain as the new cells they found in the mice: the hippocampus.

Incredibly, it was possible to ascertain that the new brain cells were only about a month old, meaning that they had formed while the donor was dying from a serious illness – not even cancer could stop the brain from creating new cells! It was visible through the microscope that the new cells had made connections with older brain cells and appeared to have integrated into the hippocampus, meaning they had assimilated into their new environment. It's likely that they functioned and had been useful while the patient was still alive.

The significance of the donors' brains containing newly created brain cells was enormous. The phenomenal discovery that neurogenesis – the creation and development of new cells in the brain – occurs in the adult human brain made headlines all over the world. Medical textbooks had to be rewritten. The 'truth' that brain cells can't regenerate over a lifetime was proven false.

However, as is so often the case in the world of scientific research, one answered question usually begets new unanswered ones. Now the big question was: does regeneration of cells happen at the same rate no matter how you live your life, and if not, what influences it? Is it possible to speed up this regeneration, and if so, how? One reasonable area of focus would be the influence of physical activity, since studies already showed that it provided the best results in mice.

So is this it? Do we know for sure that exercise leads to a higher rate of brain cell regeneration, even in humans? And do we improve our memory by being physically active? The answer to both those questions is yes. At least, that's the conclusion reached after two decades of research conducted since the discovery of human neurogenesis.

THE MIND-BODY METHOD

Atomic weapons testing could answer the question

Before we continue, let's ask the following question: how important is the regeneration of new brain cells in the hippocampus? Is it something that is only visible in laboratory experiments but lacks practical significance? To start, the regeneration of brain cells is far from insignificant! Approximately *one-third* of all the cells in the hippocampus are replaced by new cells over our lifetime.

So how do we know this? When the brain of a deceased person is examined, you can't tell whether the cells were made when the person was an adult or whether they were there when the person was born. The methods used by Fred Gage and Peter Eriksson only revealed whether the cells had been created recently – after BrdU was introduced in the body – and would not show if the cells had been created at any point in one's life prior to the injection of BrdU. To solve this mystery, scientists at Sweden's Karolinska Institute used something we might not immediately associate with neuroscience: detonations of atomic weapons.

A number of detonations were performed during the Cold War in the 1950s and 1960s, many of them in far-flung islands in the Pacific Ocean. Even though the tests took place on the other side of the globe, the radioactive isotope C-14 got into the atmosphere and spread over the whole planet. Since then, the concentration of C-14 in the atmosphere has been measured regularly, so we know how much of it has been in the air over the years.

So what does this have to do with brain cells? Well, every time a new brain cell is generated, new DNA is created, and with it C-14 at the same concentration as was present in the atmosphere the year the cell was generated; it's built right into the DNA's helix. This means you can date a cell by comparing its concentration of C-14 with the atmospheric concentration at the time. A 45-year-old brain cell in a 45-year-old man will have been there since his birth, while a 30-year-old brain cell in the same man must have been formed when he was a teenager.

By using this method, it is possible to date hippocampus cells in deceased donors who were up to 90 years old when they passed away. One can then calculate how many cells were the same age as the donor and how many were younger. This is exactly what the Karolinska reasearchers did and the results showed that almost one-third of the cells in the hippocampus had concentrations of C-14 in their DNA that indicated that they must have been created after birth. In fact, the tests showed that 1,400 new cells are generated in the hippocampus of an adult brain every day. This means that every minute of every hour of every day of your adult life a new cell is created in your hippocampus.

New cells are important for our wellbeing

Research hasn't only been able to show that large numbers of new cells are created in the hippocampus over your entire life; it has also shown that regeneration of cells strengthens memory and is pivotal to mental wellbeing. Many believe that depression is an illness caused by poor nerve cell regeneration, and that the lack of new cells is the true *cause* of depression.

A clue to this hypothesis is that antidepressant medication boosts the regeneration of brain cells. If you block the brain's ability to create new cells, it will render the antidepressants useless and the depression will not clear. In other words, a person becomes unresponsive to antidepressants if the brain can't create new cells. This strongly suggests that regeneration of brain cells is critical to our sense of wellbeing and to our ability to recover from depression. If our ability to generate new brain cells decreases, we may start feeling low, become depressed and exhibit poorer memory. In contrast, we know that being active can double our brain cell regeneration rate; it truly has that much of an impact.

Move more and develop a more nuanced world view

The hippocampus, our memory centre, is made up of several parts, and neurogenesis happens primarily in one of these parts: the dentate gyrus. It's interesting that the production of brain cells happens right in that spot. The dentate gyrus has a very specific function: it is important for what is called 'pattern separation', the ability to register small, subtle differences in what is happening around you, compared to earlier events. Let's say you enter a room where a cocktail party is in full swing. One of the guests is your sister, a few are close friends of yours, and a few others are casual acquaintances you have only met a few times. Some people you've never met before.

When you see your sister, you recognise her immediately. Your brain doesn't have to work very hard to identify her. The same goes with your friends. However, when you see people you've only met once or twice, your brain begins matching their faces to the information in your memory bank. *Who is that? Don't I know her? She looks like someone from my old job, but no – that's not her, because she was taller and had lighter hair.*

When you are thinking as hard as you possibly can to remember someone in front of you, your dentate gyrus is working on overdrive to match the face with memories of people you've met before. By sifting through minute differences in, say, hair colour, height or facial features, the dentate gyrus is trying to decide whether you know this person. They can remind you of someone else, and it is by noticing the little details that you'll know if this is someone you have met before or if they are a stranger.

Much of what we experience resembles things that we have previously been through. Think back over what you've done today.

How many activities were truly unique, things you've never done before? Probably not many, unless you live a very varied life.

Even though many things that happen to us remind us of things we've done before, and many people we meet remind us of others we've crossed paths with, the brain has to store information on similar events and people as separate memories that can be told apart. That's what pattern separation is; it is a crucial ability for us to have a nuanced view of our environment. Without it, our memories would just merge together into a fog and render us incapable of telling one from the other. Consequently, the regeneration of cells happens in the part of the brain that is important for pattern separation. Thus you can assertively claim – especially if you are physically active – that exercising improves your odds of having a more nuanced world view.

Personally I believe this could be why physical activity is so effective at treating depression. A person suffering from depression leads a reduced emotional life; they end up missing out on life's little subtleties and they feel that things are grey and dreary. The opportunities to catch a more nuanced glance at life – and glimmers of hope – increase thanks to the regeneration of brain cells in the dentate gyrus.

Does only exercise count?

Does only exercise count for increasing the regeneration of brain cells? Are more stimulating surroundings – i.e. an enriched environment – also important to the brain's ability to create new cells? Yes, the environment plays a role. How many new cells we make doesn't only depend on how many cells are created, but also on how many of those cells we get to keep. New brain cells are incredibly fragile; barely one in two survive. However, it looks like it's possible to raise the odds of survival so that more of them make it. For animals in an enriched environment, about 80 per cent of new brain cells remain viable.

Exercise and physical activity favour the creation of additional brain cells, and a stimulating environment increases the odds that those cells will survive. It's logical that these two are linked: we have evolved to experience new environments and events as we move about. This means the brain is prepared to take in new information. To increase our ability to remember what we experience, new cells are created in the hippocampus. Then what we experience as we move around (i.e. the new environment) provides the stimulation that ensures the survival of these cells.

So, to sum up: exercise and physical training lay the groundwork for the brain to learn new things. Is it beginning to seem less strange that we can recall up to 20 per cent more words if we walk while we listen to them? I thought so.

WHAT ELSE IS INVOLVED IN REGENERATING BRAIN CELLS?

Besides exercise, sex, a low-calorie diet (but not starvation) and the flavonoids found in, among other things, plain chocolate are all associated with an increase in the neurogenesis rate of new brain cells. A decrease in new cells can be caused by stress, lack of sleep, too much alcohol and a high-fat diet, especially one high in the saturated fats found in butter and cheese.

Our inbuilt emotional brake and GPS

The hippocampus helps us build long-term memories, but its responsibilities don't end there. The hippocampus is also important for our ability to put things into perspective, and to compare what we're currently experiencing with other memories so we don't overreact emotionally. Furthermore, it plays an important role in our ability to place ourselves spatially, like a 'brain GPS' that keeps track of our position and allows us to store memories of places (a discovery that was awarded the Nobel Prize in Medicine in 2014, by the way). As you read this, specific cells in your hippocampus are signalling where in the room – or outside – you are located. If you move a few inches, other hippocampus cells that function as 'place cells' become active and create an inner map of your surroundings.

In other words, the hippocampus has a list of important functions other than being a memory centre, such as controlling our emotions, keeping track of us spatially and making sure we can find our way around locations we've been in before. The more we learn about the hippocampus, the more we realise its importance. If the hippocampus doesn't work, neither does the brain.

There is a reason why I've devoted so many pages to describing the hippocampus: because it's probably the part of the brain that is most influenced by us moving our bodies.

Physical activity leads to the birth of new cells in the hippocampus. The hippocampus gets more energy when blood flow increases, so it functions better. Also, the existing hippocampus cells seem to become genetically younger, and the shrinking that occurs with ageing can be slowed down, perhaps even turned around. Over the long haul, the hippocampus – and therefore the whole brain – works better and more effectively in people who exercise regularly.

Many who train find that they make quicker and better associations – they think quicker on their feet.

Those of you who train will notice that the hippocampus is strengthened in several different ways. Aside from your memory improving, you will eventually notice that you're better able to control your emotions and you don't react as strongly to negative events. It might also affect how well you find your way around different places. Moreover, many who train find that they make quicker and better associations – in other words, they think quicker on their feet – which could be due to having a strong hippocampus.

Different types of exercise affect different kinds of memory

Even if memories are spread out all over the brain, different areas specialise in handling different kinds of memories. The frontal lobe and the hippocampus are important for working memory, as in being able to keep a phone number in your head while you dial it. The hippocampus is also important for remembering places.

The temporal lobe is key to 'episodic memory', which is how you remember, say, the things you did on Christmas Eve. To a large extent, memories are stored in the same area that was active when the event occurred, so visual memories are stored primarily in the visual cortex.

Fascinatingly, it seems that different types of movement can influence the brain's different areas in a variety of ways. This leads us to wonder whether different types of training have an impact on different kinds of memories. For example, it has been shown that word recall is boosted by running but not by lifting weights. However, weight training appears to be good for 'associative memory', such as the ability to pair a name with a face. When it comes to remembering where you put the keys, both running and weight training seem to do the trick.

Even though this knowledge is in its infancy, we can draw two conclusions from the studies that have been done. First and most importantly, if you wish to strengthen your memory, you must be physically active in one way or another. Exactly what you choose to do is secondary. However, if you want to boost all your memory areas, from remembering where you've put stuff down to recalling the words you've read, you should vary your training and make sure you do both cardiovascular exercise and weight training. If for some reason you must choose between the two, cardio should take priority since it is generally more beneficial for memory.

That both the hippocampus and the frontal lobe are strengthened by exercise means that physical activity should be able to improve many areas of your memory; it's possible that both your short-term memory (where you remember stuff for a few minutes or hours) and your long-term memory will improve. Even if most research has focused on the effects of exercise on short-term memory, physical activity seems to boost all memory, whether it concerns what happened this morning or something that took place 20 years ago!

PHYSICAL TRAINING VS COMPUTER GAMES

If you google 'cognitive training', you'll get more than 1.8 billion results. Most are ads for apps, games and other products that purport to make your brain more effective. It is certainly a tempting offer – who doesn't want to have a better functioning brain? Training the brain has, in a very short time, become a multibillion-dollar industry; every year more than $10 billion in cognitive training games are sold.

Recently, 70 of the world's most eminent neuroscientists and psychologists, under the auspices of Stanford University and the Max Planck Institute, decided to see whether there was any merit to these game and app manufacturers' claims. The experts scoured the scientific studies on cognitive training to find answers to the question of whether games can improve cognitive abilities.

Their conclusion came in the form of scathing criticism. It was found that the cognitive training methods proffered by games and apps make you progressively better at the games themselves but do not make you smarter, more focused or more creative, and do not improve your memory. You simply get better at playing the games but the transfer to cognitive functions such as memory, attention or creativity seems to be small or non-existent. The same findings apply to crosswords and Sudokus, which are often referred to as 'brain gymnastics'. If you do crosswords, you'll get better at doing crosswords, it will have little or no effect on anything else.

By contrast, research has shown time and again that exercise and physical activity can truly strengthen all our cognitive functions. If you're still on the fence about this, it just means you haven't read this book properly! In the race between physical and cognitive exercises, physical exercise wins by a mile.

THE RIGHT PRESCRIPTION FOR IMPROVED MEMORY

- Ideally you should alternate between cardiovascular (endurance) exercise and weight training. Most of the research has focused on the effect of aerobic training on the hippocampus, but it looks like some effects on memory can only, or at least mostly, be achieved by training with weights.
- Train before or while learning something.
- Don't go all out: a walk or a light jog is all that's required.
- Train regularly. Of course, you can improve your memory with a single workout, but just like with the effects on many cognitive faculties, memory improves much more if you're patient and keep up your training over several months.

CHAPTER 6

TRAIN YOURSELF CREATIVE

The moment my legs begin to move my thoughts begin to flow.
HENRY DAVID THOREAU

THE JAPANESE AUTHOR Haruki Murakami is widely known and his books have sold millions of copies around the world. He can line up a long row of prestigious literary awards and is regularly a candidate with low odds when betting companies list candidates for the Nobel Prize for Literature. Anyone who wonders where Murakami gets his inspiration need look no further than the title of his 2008 autobiography, *What I Talk About When I Talk About Running*. In the book, Murakami describes his creative process in detail: when he is writing, he gets up at 4am and works until 10am; then he goes for a 10km (6 mile) run after lunch and follows that with a swim. He spends the rest of the day listening to music and reading. He goes to bed around 9pm. He follows this routine seven days a week for six months until the book he is working on is finished. To get things done, Murakami needs the physical strength he gets from training, which he considers as essential to the writing process as his creativity.

Murakami is far from alone in having discovered the effects exercise can have on one's creative energy. There is a slew of authors, musicians, actors, artists, scientists and entrepreneurs who have borne witness to how training can make you more creative.

IDEAS JUST TUMBLED OUT AFTER A RUN

The effect on creativity was one of the reasons I became so interested in how the brain is influenced by physical activity. I often had good ideas after I'd been out for a run or played a game of tennis. At first I thought it was just a fluke or that I had simply become more alert, but it happened time and time again, and the effect was so tangible in the hours after my exercise that I began to wonder whether the workouts were actually making me more creative. When I found out about the studies on creativity and physical activity, it became clear that what I was experiencing wasn't just a result of feeling more alert and happier.

Boost your creativity with a walk

Many highly creative people have testified to how exercise has worked wonders for their creativity. It is said that Albert Einstein discovered the theory of relativity while on a bike ride. Beethoven, one of the greatest musical geniuses who ever lived, composed three symphonies despite going deaf in his 40s. He often took a break during the day, during which he went on a long walk for inspiration. Charles Darwin took hour-long strolls around his home at Down House, on the southern outskirts of London, round a loop he called his 'thinking path'. It was during a period of extended rambling that Darwin developed his groundbreaking work *On the Origin of Species*, the most important work ever in the field of biology.

A more current example is Apple's late co-founder and CEO Steve Jobs, who held regular walking meetings because he felt they were more productive than meetings that took place around a conference room table. He seems to have inspired many of Silicon Valley's elite, such as Facebook's founder Mark Zuckerberg and Twitter's founder Jack Dorsey, to do the same.

DIFFERENT TYPES OF CREATIVITY

While these anecdotes about the beneficial influence of exercise on creativity are fascinating, they're not hard evidence for any creativity-boosting ability of physical activity. So before we can claim that physical activity can get you to 'think outside the box' – and how you can best achieve this – we need to find out what creativity is and how you test for it.

For anything to be deemed creative, it needs to be both new and meaningful. Copying someone else's work isn't particularly creative. Besides, what is created must fulfil some purpose or function, because a pointless invention isn't very creative either.

In the study of creativity and innovation, a distinction is often made between two kinds of creativity: divergent and convergent thinking. Divergent thinking is classic brainstorming: coming up with many different solutions to a problem by thinking broadly and using plenty of associations. A typical test for divergent thinking is the Alternative Uses Test and it is based on word association. For example, you're given a word like 'brick' and you are timed while you come up with as many uses for a brick as you can. To build a wall, to construct a house, to use as a paper weight or a door stop are four possible suggestions. But it isn't just the number of answers that is important but also how detailed those answers are, and how different they are from one another. Preferably, the answers should be unique and different from what participants usually suggest. However, completely unrealistic answers, like using the brick to build a space rocket, don't count.

This test might sound simplistic, but it has been shown to reflect a person's level of creativity rather accurately; I can attest to the fact that this experiment is not easy, especially when you're being timed. A big advantage of this test is that it only measures creativity and not IQ; people with high IQs don't do better than others – in fact, they often get stuck.

Convergent thinking is almost diametrically opposed to divergent thinking. Here it's not a matter of brainstorming a variety of solutions but of quickly arriving at one answer – the correct one, which often boils down to finding a common denominator. For example, you might be given three words and asked to quickly find what they have in common. Let's say 'Hyde Park', 'Big Ben' and 'Madame Tussauds'; the common factor is that they are all tourist attractions in London. In this case there is just one or a few correct answers; the rest are wrong. Convergent thinking emphasises speed and logic more than divergent thinking. Nevertheless, convergent thinking is important for creativity in artistic as well as scientific endeavours.

Give your ideas some legs

Lately, thanks to these tests, we have found scientific proof that physical activity indeed boosts creativity. One of the more interesting studies on the topic was conducted by scientists at Stanford University, in which researchers asked 176 subjects to perform several different creativity tests. Some performed the tests after having walked and others did them after resting.

The study's title, 'Give your ideas some legs: the positive effect of walking on creative thinking', provides a clue to its outcome. On average, more than four out of five test subjects performed better on the tests when they did them right after walking. The differences weren't insignificant either. The test results of those who walked just before being tested were 60 per cent better than those who did not walk, primarily in their ability to brainstorm and generate new ideas. However, convergent thinking – i.e. the ability to find the 'right' answer and/or a common denominator – did not improve. The co-author of the study, Marily Oppezzo, made the following statement: 'We do not proclaim that walks will turn you into a modern-day Michelangelo, but they can help you to get going in the initial stages of the creative process.'

Movement is more important than environment and temperament

A shift in one's surroundings is said to stimulate a different way of thinking. There could be some truth to this, of course, but the Stanford study showed that creativity improved no matter where the walk took place. Some test subjects walked outside around the university campus, while others walked inside on a treadmill where they had only a grey wall to stare at. Despite this, creativity improved in both those who walked outside and those who walked on the treadmill.

To make sure it was the walking and not the environment that made the impact on creative thinking, some of the test subjects were pushed around in wheelchairs on the campus walking path. In other words, they saw the same surroundings as those who walked outside but they were not physically active. The result? It was not the environment that affected creativity, because creativity increased much more in the group that had walked on the path compared to the group that had been wheeled along that same path. A change of environment did not appear to have any effect on creativity. So what matters is primarily *that* we walk or run, not *where* we do it.

What about mood? Since our mood improves after physical activity, increased creativity could be explained by the fact that those who train feel better overall. However, that doesn't seem to be the case. When subjects not only did creativity tests after exercise but filled out questionnaires on how they felt, one saw that even the subjects who did not feel better after training still performed better on the test. Thus, improved creativity is not the result of simply feeling better.

In other words, fresh ideas are linked to physical activity and cannot be explained by extenuating circumstances such as a change in environment or mood.

Should you run or walk?

The test subjects of the Stanford University study walked around the campus, but what is optimal for increasing creativity – should you walk or should you run? Even if it isn't entirely possible to say for sure, one could postulate that running, or moving in an equally vigorous way, is better than walking. Making a little more of an effort does seem to pay off, but you need to keep it up for at least 30 minutes. Improved creativity expresses itself mainly *after* training, which is obviously more practical since we likely don't want to brainstorm and take notes while walking, and certainly not while running.

How long do we remain creative after moving around? Does it last for the rest of our life, or at least for the rest of the day? Sadly, no. The creative boost is quite short-lived; it increases for about one hour after exertion and then it wears off. If we want another jolt of inspiration, we must go for another walk or run, just like Haruki Murakami and his daily runs. However, from a creative standpoint, it is unwise to go all out to the point of exhaustion because that will not improve creativity. In fact, experiments have demonstrated that people who push too hard tend to perform worse on creativity tests after their workouts.

We do not yet know why the benefits are so short-lived and why they disappear if we become too fatigued. One possible explanation could be that blood flow to the brain increases when we move around. When the brain gets more blood it works more efficiently and our cognitive abilities – among them, creativity – improve. But if we work out to the point of exhaustion, blood flow to the brain decreases instead. Blood is now redirected from the brain to the muscles, where it is needed to provide us with maximum performance.

Less blood in the brain seems to lead to lower mental capabilities. Maybe there have been times you've had a hard time thinking clearly when you've been exhausted? Be that as it may, it's important to emphasise that the dip in creativity that follows fatigue is only temporary; nothing suggests creativity dwindles over the long term due to hard training.

Make sure to start out fit

Does everyone become more creative by exercising? No, there is a catch: you need to be reasonably fit already to see good results. Fit people actually perform better on creativity tests if they are done in tandem with physical activity. Creativity doesn't seem to improve at all in people who are not fit; in fact, it seems to worsen a few hours after training, at least if the training session was intense. This is probably from the decrease in blood flow to the brain due to exhaustion; even a short run at an unhurried pace can be exhausting for an unfit individual.

So if you want to boost your creativity by exercising, you need to make sure you're in reasonably good shape to start seeing positive outcomes. If you're not at that point yet but still wish to strengthen your creativity by training, it's best to walk or jog at a leisurely pace so you don't drain your tanks completely.

Ingenuity or hard work?

In a letter, Mozart explained how he composed his music. The process cannot be described as anything but pure magic. The legendary composer created his musical masterpieces without even going near an instrument: he heard complete pieces in his head and then he simply wrote them down, as if they had already been composed. Later, when his work was performed by a symphony orchestra, the music sounded as wonderful as when he had first heard it in his head.

This image of an artistic genius's enormous creative powers is undoubtedly compelling, and it's often used to illustrate how the brains of extremely creative people work in ways we mere mortals can scarcely imagine. The problem is the letter is a fake.* Mozart didn't compose his symphonies that way at all. Everything suggests he worked with determination, and he used music theory as well as other established methods to write. He spent endless hours fine-tuning his pieces, reworking them, modifying and reworking them again until he was satisfied. Mozart's classical masterpieces seem to have been the product of hard work rather than eureka moments.

There is a similar story about how Newton arrived at his theory of gravity – just like that, when an apple fell on his head while he was sitting under a tree. What is not recounted, however, is the decades he spent toiling in mathematics and physics before the idea struck him, and that it took 20 years from the apple incident for Newton's complete theory to be fully articulated.

Of course, Mozart and Newton might have had their 'Eureka!' moments, but it is likely that their flashes of brilliance didn't hit them haphazardly, but were instead the product of a long and painstaking slog. This doesn't mean everyone who makes the effort can compose

* That Mozart's letter is a forgery is shown in Kevin Ashton's *How to Fly a Horse*.

timeless music like Mozart, or make trailblazing contributions to science like Newton, but it certainly means we can all practise and fine-tune our creative abilities if we try.

Quantity leads to quality

Do you belong to that category of people who come up with plenty of ideas, make free associations left, right and centre, and suggest one thing after another when brainstorming? Or are you one of those people who only suggest a few things and hope they'll be good enough? The first process has proven to be the best way to come up with the best ideas.

When you become physically and mentally stronger through physical activity, your stamina for work increases, too.

When we study how people perform on creativity tests for divergent thinking, those who have lots of ideas also tend to have a greater number of *good* ideas. This may sound obvious, but it's worth looking closer at the implications. If you generate a lot of ideas, it's more likely you will hit upon a good one, even if the rest are bad. It's not as common to come up with only one or two brilliant ideas with no throwaways.

For most of us to think up more ideas, we must put in more effort. That importance of perseverance in creativity is underrated, as evidenced by the fictional tales of Mozart and Newton. Exercise isn't beneficial just for divergent and convergent thinking, but also for having the energy to keep plugging away. When you become physically and mentally stronger through physical activity, your stamina for work increases, too – as exemplified by Haruki Murakami during his intense bouts of writing – and so good ideas tend to pop up sooner or later.

HOW CREATIVITY WORKS

Our awareness about what happens in the brain when we're being creative has advanced by leaps and bounds; we no longer consider the creative process some sort of 'black box' about which little is known.

We have begun to understand *why* some people are more creative than others. Researchers on creativity have not only directed their interest towards areas of the brain like the frontal lobes (the seat of our higher cognitive functions); the trail also seems to lead to an area deeper inside the brain: the thalamus.

The thalamus sorts out information

You brain is analysing an enormous amount of information at this very moment: what you're seeing and hearing, how your arms and legs are positioned, whether it's warm or cold in the room, how your lungs fill with air as you breathe and how quickly your heart is beating. Your brain receives this information continuously, day and night. We're conscious of some of this data and unaware of the rest. We typically don't give much thought to our breathing or our leg placement, and it must be this way for us to function normally. If all this information reached our consciousness, we wouldn't be able to concentrate on anything besides our initial impressions.

The thalamus is the part of the brain that acts as a kind of filter for our consciousness, to prevent us from becoming overwhelmed by information. As we've already learned, the thalamus is situated in the brain like the hub of a bicycle wheel, where all the spokes meet; it's not by accident that the thalamus is located so centrally. Information is gathered in the thalamus from the brain's different areas (e.g. the centres for visual impressions), at which point it chooses which signals to let through to our consciousness. The thalamus is like an executive assistant who picks which meetings the boss – in this case, the cerebral cortex and our consciousness – should attend, and which ones they can sit out. If the thalamus doesn't function properly, the cerebral cortex runs the risk of becoming overloaded with information and not working as it should. In effect, the indecisive assistant inundates the boss with meetings, and consequently they can't actually get anything done.

To 'think outside the box'

Today we believe that this kind of information overload is what happens in the psychiatric disorder we call schizophrenia, where the sufferer loses touch with reality and experiences symptoms such as delusions and visual and auditory hallucinations. Much evidence points to the schizophrenic's brain receiving too many strong impressions at once, making it hard for them to hang on to the real world. This leads the afflicted individual to subconsciously create an alternative picture of their surroundings. Individuals suffering from schizophrenia often exhibit very bizarre thought patterns; I have met some who cling to such weird delusions, and I could never have made thought associations along those same lines, no matter how hard I tried.

But there are always two sides to a coin. Having a thalamus that lets through a lot of information isn't always a weakness or something that leads to mental illness. It also appears to be related to creativity; it can lead us to make unexpected associations and 'think outside the box'. If our cerebral cortex and consciousness receive many signals, this increases our chances of having unique ideas and seeing things from a different perspective than most people.

So how does our brain work? For the thalamus filter to function normally, we need dopamine (yes, even here it plays an important role!), but not too much of it and not too little – just enough. If dopamine levels deviate from the correct amount, the thalamus might not let the right number of signals through; this could lead to information overload, which can be either a benefit or a drawback.

In other words, this indicates that dopamine levels in the thalamus could be linked to creativity *and* mental illness. This in fact appears to be the case. We know from experiments performed by Swedish professor and neuroscientist Fredrik Ullén at the Karolinska Institute that people who perform especially well on creativity tests for divergent thinking have fewer dopamine receptors in the thalamus. As a consequence, their thalamus lets through more signals and their thinking is more creative.

What's interesting is that the same thing has been observed in individuals with schizophrenia who perform well on creativity tests: they seem to have fewer dopamine receptors in the thalamus, but for them this leads to psychosis instead of creative thinking. So what decides whether we'll become mentally ill or a creative genius? We don't know for sure right now, but maybe if our brain works well in other ways, then the increased flow of information becomes an asset instead of a liability. It could be that the brain is resilient enough to handle the strain of added data without having to resort to creating alternative realities. You may be original and creative and able to think in unusual ways and come up with original ideas no one else could have thought about without becoming psychotic. However, if your brain is not that strong at processing a vast flow of information, it won't be able to handle the deluge of information and so you could suffer from psychosis and lose touch with reality.

When it comes to the brain, things are seldom black and white, where you either possess an ability or you don't. There are grey zones in which you can show signs of certain qualities but to different extents. It isn't that people who let a large load of information through the thalamus are either creative or psychotic. There is a vast spectrum between creativity and mental illness along which people are situated. Some may have to deal with an intense flow of information through the thalamus, and their brain hangs on for dear life to cope with the load. At certain times in their lives they may show symptoms bordering on psychosis, while at other times, when their brain is running smoothly, they can create things others can only dream about.

A hairline fissure separates madness from genius

There are many individuals throughout history who have shown us how close creativity is to madness. Two of the most famous are the artist Vincent van Gogh and the philosopher Friedrich Nietzsche, who were both enormously creative yet also suffered from mental illness at different points in their lives. A later example is the Nobel Prize winner for Economics John Nash, who combined exceptional creativity with severe mental illness. Nash, portrayed by Russell Crowe in the Oscar-winning movie *A Beautiful Mind*, was one of the world's leading mathematicians, and he also happened to suffer from schizophrenia. He heard voices and was delusional, believing that he was being followed, threatened and conspired against. He found his affliction to be both a blessing and a curse. 'I would never have had such good scientific ideas had I been able to think normally,' he said about his exceptional creative abilities.

Many highly creative people don't suffer from mental illness themselves, but they can trace it in their families. One of the greatest minds of our age, Albert Einstein, had a son who was schizophrenic. Polymath Bertrand Russell, a philosopher, an author and a politician, had many relatives who suffered from schizophrenia. The endlessly creative David Bowie had a schizophrenic brother.

One possible explanation for this link is that both the creative people and their afflicted relatives had a greater flow of information through the thalamus – a more intense thought flow – but some of them had brains that could handle the excess data and knew how to make use of it. This is what made them geniuses, while their relatives, who had less resilient brains, became mentally ill.

Boost the flow of ideas and your ability to handle them

The frontal lobe seems to be vital for channelling the flow of ideas through the thalamus and making something out of them. As we've already seen, exercise strengthens the frontal lobe. It does this in the short term by increasing blood flow and thus making the frontal lobe work better, and over the long term through other mechanisms which I discuss in Chapter 3. This could mean that exercise improves the conditions for using our flow of ideas and turning them into something productive.

In addition, exercise doesn't merely affect our ability to handle the flow of ideas, it is also likely to influence the flow of ideas itself. We're not sure exactly what mechanisms are responsible for this, but one possibility is that physical activity affects dopamine, which is critical to the 'filter' in the thalamus. However, it's not always the case that more – or less – dopamine is always better. The systems in the brain are incredibly complex, and theories about having too much or too little of one thing or another are often far too simplistic. Instead, one way to look at it is that the different systems are more or less in tune, and exercise fine-tunes the dopamine system, influencing how you feel and how much information the thalamus lets through, thereby affecting how creative you are.

Are you stuck on a problem at work? Are you having trouble finding a good idea for a book to write or a company to launch? If so, get out there and run!

We're born with an individual range of basic creative talent, and we can't change that. What we do with that talent, however, is up to us. There are many different factors that are important for creativity, but the fact is that physical activity is one of the most important. Are you stuck on a problem at work? Are you having trouble finding a good idea for a book to write or a company to launch? If so, get out there and run! If it can work wonders for Haruki Murakami and Beethoven, it should also be able to help you and me.

THE RIGHT PRESCRIPTION TO INCREASE CREATIVITY

- The best way to boost creativity is to go for a run or get active in a similarly vigorous way. A walk is good, too, but it won't be as effective.
- Run for at least 20–30 minutes. You'll feel the effect on your creativity afterwards and it will last for about an hour, so use that hour constructively.
- Don't run to the point of exhaustion, because creativity diminishes for several hours after a hard workout (not over the long term, though).
- Make sure you're fit already, because that is when the effect of exercise on creativity is strongest.
- Training primarily improves the ability to *brainstorm*, but that might differ from person to person.

CHAPTER 7

THE GROWING BRAIN

Intelligence and skills can only function at the peak
of their capacity when the body is healthy and strong.

JOHN F. KENNEDY

THE PROGRAM FOR International Student Assessment (PISA) measures the scholastic performance of 15-year-olds and is used to compare the academic prowess of students across different countries. In December 2013, the results of the PISA were presented, and they shocked the population of my home nation, Sweden. Swedish students weren't just lightyears behind places like South Korea, Singapore and Hong Kong, which topped the list, but they also performed worse than average compared to other countries in the Organisation for Economic Cooperation and Development. Sweden also came last out of all the Nordic countries. Science, maths and reading levels were especially dire; Sweden was heading in the wrong direction.

Lively debates ensued and many people had ideas about how to turn this situation around. But maybe the discussion should centre less on teaching methods and class size, and more on research that has shown that being physically active has a formidable influence on children's memory and learning abilities. Today, children simply do not get enough physical education.

It isn't just what happens when children sit in class that affects their development; research has clearly shown that movement reinforces children's and teenagers' ability to learn. School sports are about so much more than what takes place on the football field or in the gymnasium. It's definitely not about making children good at certain sports; it's about improving the groundwork for learning maths and languages, among other subjects.

MORE GYM CLASSES, HIGHER GRADES

The most convincing proof that exercise improves children's academic results in the 'three Rs' – reading, 'riting and 'rithmetic – has come from Bunkeflo, a suburb in the southern region of Skåne in Sweden. Two primary school classes were followed as they participated in gym sessions every day, while another class at the same school (the control group) engaged in the typical two sessions per week.

The groups of children were comparable in every respect other than the level of sports activity they took part in: they all lived in the same area, attended the same school and studied the same subjects. So what happened? For starters, those who went to the gym every day got better grades in gym class than the others – no surprise there. What was unexpected, however, was that they also did better in their maths, Swedish and English classes, without getting any extra tutoring in these subjects. And the effects continued over many years; even though these kids only had extra gym classes in primary school, many of them graduated from ninth grade (Year 10) with satisfactory grades. The effect was especially noticeable among the boys. Typically, girls get better grades than boys, but the grades levelled out completely between the genders in the children who participated in a daily gym class. No other approach has provided this kind of outcome.

It's not only in Skåne in southern Sweden that we've seen this link between exercise and academic achievement: American scientists also noticed it when they studied some 250 primary school children in grades 3 and 5 (Years 4 and 6). The scientists measured cardiovascular fitness, muscle strength and agility to paint a complete picture of the participants' physical fitness. They also looked at how well the children did academically. Here, too, the results were unambiguous: physically fit children did better at maths and reading comprehension. The higher their fitness levels, the higher their grades. The opposite was true for overweight children, who typically had worse test scores. The widely held preconception that overweight children are academically minded and physically active children are empty-headed was proven to be completely baseless.

But we must be careful when drawing conclusions from studies of only a couple of hundred children. Is there more data that supports these conclusions? There certainly is. In Nebraska, nearly 10,000 children were tested, and the fitter children tested better in maths and English than those who were unfit. However, excess weight – a major concern in the US – didn't play a role in the findings. Overweight children scored neither better nor worse than children of normal weight.

So how can exercise make children better at maths and English? As we discovered in Chapter 5, physical activity makes the hippocampus – the centre for memory and emotional control – grow in physically active adults. This appears to happen in children, too.

When the brains of 10-year-olds were examined by MRI, it was found that fit children had bigger hippocampi. Thus, one of the most important areas of the brain is also bigger in fit children. It is theoretically possible that fit children have had a bigger hippocampus from the beginning, and that the physical activity had nothing to do with it. However, that is not likely, since fit children not only had a bigger hippocampus but also did better on memory tests. So good physical fitness does indeed seem to lead to both a larger hippocampus *and* better results on memory tests.

What's more, the more complex the tests, the bigger the difference between the fit and unfit children. On simple memory tests the differences were small or non-existent, but on difficult tests the fit children did much better.

When nine-year-olds were physically active for 20 minutes, they became markedly better at reading. One short burst of exercise altered the kids' academic abilities!

A single training session produces results

Just as exercise has an immediate impact on the adult brain, the same rapid strengthening takes effect in children's brains. When nine-year-olds were physically active for 20 minutes – in one single session – they became markedly better at reading. One short burst of exercise improved the children's academic abilities. Why this happens we don't know for sure, but we are certain that children's attention spans improve immediately after they are physically active, so we can assume that attention span has an important role to play in this context.

Just as we've examined the minimum amount of training required for adults to see an improvement in fitness, we've also

　　　THE MIND-BODY METHOD

checked to see how little training is needed to improve the attention spans of children. The results are astonishing! When teenagers jogged for 12 minutes, both their reading comprehension and their 'visual attention' – meaning the ability to select what visual information one should focus on and not be distracted by anything else – improved. The effect lasted the better part of an hour. Even a bout of activity as brief as four minutes (yes, you read that right!) can improve children's ability to stay focused, alert and remain undistracted!

Attention span and memory are not the only things that improve in physically active children. Today we know that physically active kids between the ages of 4 and 18 will show improvement in practically *all* their cognitive faculties. Multitasking, working memory and focus – everything seems to get better. The same goes for the ability to make decisions, i.e. executive control.

Executive control might sound like a trait only company directors need to have. However, even children need to be able to show initiative and make decisions. They need to be able to plan, organise and stay focused on what they are doing, even when they're being distracted by, say, their mobile phone. Children must also be able to stop themselves from giving in to every single impulse they feel. Thus, it's not exactly rash to say that executive control is necessary to do well academically.

Less stressed children

The effects of being physically active in childhood have repercussions that go far beyond academic success and proper executive control. Children also become less sensitive to stress. A study of 258 Finnish nine-year-olds examined how they reacted to stressful situations and whether there was a connection between their vulnerability to stress and their level of physical activity. Asking such young children how physically active they are does not yield reliable answers, so the kids were given pedometers. Their stress resilience was measured through tests that mimicked daily stressors in school, such as being timed while doing arithmetic or giving presentations to each other – situations that are just as stressful for children as for adults.

It turned out that children who took a lot of steps every day didn't react as strongly to stress as the kids who didn't walk as much. Put simply: the physically active children handled stress better, and this didn't just show in their calmer demeanour: the levels of the stress hormone cortisol didn't rise as much in the physically active children as in the sedentary kids when they completed high-stress arithmetic and presentation tests. This is evidence that physically active children are more resilient to stress.

I completely understand how one can feel guilty when reading about these studies, especially if you have children who aren't interested in sports and are glued to their phones and computers. How do you go about getting them to be active? A good starting point is to let your child pick what they enjoy doing. Scientists in the US tried this by letting overweight primary school children, who were not into sports and were mostly sedentary in their free time, get together and be physically active after school. To get the children to join in, they let them choose an activity they thought would be fun, so long as they did something.

Some kids ran, some skipped and some played ball sports. The result? The kids improved in maths without having to take extra lessons. The more physically active they became, the more their maths scores improved, even though they hadn't completed any extra class work. Twenty short minutes of exercise produced results, but the kids who saw the most improvement were active for at least 40 minutes and increased their heart rate substantially, preferably up to 150bpm.

But the positive effects didn't stop at improved maths comprehension. A few of the overweight children who did not like sports

THE MIND-BODY METHOD

but were encouraged to become active were examined by MRI. The images showed that activity in their prefrontal cortex – the area behind the forehead, our centre for abstract thinking, concentration and planning – had increased. The study's authors summarised this finding: 'For children to reach their full potential, they need to be active.'

In the short and the long term

When we fit the pieces of this puzzle together, the amazing effect that exercise has on children's brains becomes obvious, both in the short and the long term. A single bout of activity increases attention span and improves concentration and reading comprehension. It continues to do so for up to several hours and then it wears off. Like adults, children reap significant, long-term benefits if they train regularly for several months. Again, as with adults, the choice of activity is not really important; running, playing sports and competing in tennis or football all seem to have the same positive impact. What is vital is raising the heart rate. The critical thing is not *what* the children do to be physically active, it's that they *are* physically active.

From the perspective of brain development, is there an age at which we should be especially mindful that our kids exercise? We don't know in detail yet, but several clues suggest children of primary school age reap the most benefits from being active.

Training strengthens different areas in a child's brain

We know how physical activity strengthens the adult brain. We also know that a child's brain changes with physical activity, and we know what happens inside the brain. But let us look closer at the effects on the two different types of matter in the brain: grey and white matter.

Grey matter, also known as the cerebral cortex, is the brain's outermost layer. It is a few millimetres thick and it isn't grey but more pink due to all the blood vessels there that provide the brain with blood. It's in the grey matter that sophisticated activity takes place; information is sorted and memories are stored. All the energy grey matter consumes shows us that this is where the 'magic' happens. It uses more than 90 per cent of the brain's total energy, even though it only makes up about 40 per cent of the volume.

White matter lies beneath grey matter and passes information between different areas of the brain. It's made up of long projections (called axons) from the nerve cells, which the brain cells use to communicate with one another. Imagine grey matter as a bunch of computers and white matter as the cables that pass signals between them.

The pale colour of white matter comes from the axons it is made up of, which are insulated with a substance called myelin that contains a lot of fat. Myelin improves the signal transmission between the brain cells.

Both grey and white matter are vital to how we function. Grey matter performs most of the heavy lifting, but if the axons aren't effective and can't transmit signals, the brain won't work properly. That makes sense – a computer can only run if all its parts are properly connected.

So what changes most in children who are physically active: grey or white matter? Both! Growth of grey matter is first seen in the hippocampus, but white matter is also strengthened by exercise. Children who are regularly physically active show changes in their white matter, which becomes thicker and more compact. This almost certainly means that it's becoming more efficient. In science, this is called better 'white matter integrity'.

To return to the idea of white matter as cables between computers, it appears that these connections work better in physically active children. This means that information is transmitted more efficiently between different areas of the brain, making the entire brain run better.

There's no doubt that grey matter is essential to cognitive ability, but it looks like the same goes for white matter, too. In fact, white matter has been specifically linked to academic performance. When primary school children's brains were examined by diffusion tensor imaging – an advanced medical imaging technique – the scans showed that white matter in the left side of the brain is related to mathematical ability. We can't say for sure if it's the strengthening of the white matter that makes fit children do better in school, but there are good reasons to believe it helps.

Interestingly, the benefits of training on white matter don't just affect children. Exercise seems to improve white matter in people of any age. There is a very strong correlation between white matter in older people and how active they are. The greatest effect on white matter doesn't come from heavy-duty exercise but rather from everyday activity and not sitting too much. Again: there's no need to run marathons.

Better gamer if you move

If your child prefers spending time in front of the computer and you are in desperate need for an argument to convince him or her to go for a walk or run, I have one ace up my sleeve: you will become a better gamer if you are physically active!

The online game *League of Legends* is played by more than 180 million players, and since the game is such a phenomenon there are many competitions, some with serious prize money. Players often train hard to become better at the game, some really hard. In 2019, a study was presented where experienced

League of Legends players who played on average 11 hours per week were randomised into two groups. One group did intense and pulse-raising exercise for 15 minutes before they played the game. The other group rested for 15 minutes before they played. The result? The exercise group performed 10 per cent better. That may not sound much but remember, these were all really good players. At that level, an additional improvement of 10 per cent is the difference between being really good and being the best, so for all gamers: you will perform at the top of your game if you take the time to be physically active!

You think better on your feet

It has become popular to use standing desks at the office. For most people, the biggest reason to stand is probably to burn extra calories while they're working. It is true that you use more energy when standing compared to sitting – almost twice as much – but increased calorie expenditure is a benefit that is outshone by what happens in the brain. The main benefit of standing, whether you're at school or at work, is that the brain functions slightly better when you stand.

When the academic performance of seventh-graders (Year 8s) was measured using a series of cognitive tests, the kids showed clearer focus and had better working memory and executive control after they started using standing desks at school. The tests measured qualities that are essential for getting good grades, such as reading comprehension, memorisation of facts and the ability to solve problems in several steps. The differences were significant: the test results indicated an average improvement of 10 per cent. Not a big difference, but not insignificant either.

Naturally, the authors weren't satisfied with only using cognitive tests; they also scanned the students' brains with MRI. (My guess is that you might be noticing a pattern in these types of studies by now:

first there are mental tests, then there are MRI examinations to see how the brain works). The test results might even start to look familiar: children who had been standing before the scan had increased activity in the areas of their frontal lobe that are essential for working memory and concentration.

We see the same type of result in children who stand in class – increased activity in the frontal lobe, meaning better working memory and better focus – as in adults and children who run, walk or are otherwise physically active. The conclusion is simple: we literally think better on our feet! At school, children who stand are better at concentrating and learning.

SMART JOCKS

Just a few years ago, not many people believed that children's and adults' brains could change so dramatically by engaging in physical activity. Exercise makes us feel better and tolerate stress better. It improves our memory and makes us more creative and focused – abilities we commonly refer to as cognitive or mental. The collective measure of all our cognitive abilities is our intelligence. So if our cognitive abilities are strengthened by movement, then training should increase our IQ, but is this the case? Can training make us smarter? If so, it would almost be too good to be true.

Scientists attempted to answer this question as early as the 1960s, but it proved to be easier said than done. The main snag is that we don't know what comes first: if tests suggest that fit people are also highly intelligent, we don't know if it's the activity that has made them smarter, or if naturally smart people are more likely to exercise. Furthermore, you would need to study *many* individuals to make sure that the results are representative of the whole population.

Data from more than 1 million Swedish men was crucial to solving this mystery. Up to 2010, military service was compulsory for all

Swedish 18-year-old males. Over the course of one trying day, a battery of tests were performed on Sweden's newest recruits – myself included some 25 years ago. Among other things, their endurance was measured by having the recruits pedal to the point of failure on an exercise bike on which the resistance was continually increased. It was incredibly hard and I remember barely being able to stand after getting off the bike. Tests on muscle strength came next, then a psychological evaluation, and the induction day ended with an IQ test.

Over 26 years, more than 1.2 million 18-year-olds took these tests. When the results were compiled recently, a clear pattern cropped up: young men who were physically fit were, on average, smarter. Those who performed well on the cardiovascular fitness test had a better score on their IQ test than recruits who were less fit.

Does training make us intelligent?

Upon learning that, it is natural to think, *Wow! They became smarter by exercising!* Yes, that is possible, but let's play the devil's advocate for a moment: was it the exercise that made the young men smart, or could it simply be that the smart recruits liked to exercise more than the others? To answer this question, the scientists looked at sets of identical twins. If there's one factor more than any other that can explain your IQ, it's your parents' IQs, because intelligence is, to a high degree, inherited. Identical twins have an almost identical set of genes and, more often than not, have grown up together. When identical twins take IQ tests, their scores are typically very similar to each other. Among the million or so military recruits tested in the study, there were 1,432 pairs of identical twins. In some cases, one twin was fit while the other was not. As identical twins, they should have had similar IQs, but they didn't. The fit twin generally scored better on the IQ test than his less fit brother. Remarkably, fitness went hand in hand with better results on the IQ test, even among identical twins. That is probably the closest we can get to evidence that exercise makes us a bit smarter.

Isn't it amazing that training can make children and adults smarter?

But it's endurance – not strength – that is associated with higher scores on an IQ test. The muscular recruits did not have better results. The IQ tests measured several types of intelligence, such as vocabulary comprehension, mathematical and logical reasoning, and the ability to visualise how three-dimensional objects looked from different angles. High cardiovascular fitness was correlated with better results in all types of intelligence. The strongest correlation, however, was between high fitness and greater logic and vocabulary comprehension.

Today we know that there are two areas of the brain that are especially important for logical thinking and vocabulary comprehension: the hippocampus and the frontal lobe. That the correlation was especially strong in those areas ties in neatly with the fact that exercise's strongest effect seems to be on the hippocampus and the frontal lobe.

Higher salary and less depression later in life

The information on the Swedish military recruits has proven to be a real goldmine for scientists in search of fascinating correlations. For example, they discovered that being fit at 18 was correlated with higher educational achievement and better jobs with higher salaries at around 40 years of age. Fit young men also suffered lower rates of depression, and the incidence of severe depression also seemed to be lower because fewer subjects in the high-fit group committed or attempted to commit suicide later in life. As if the absence of mental disorders wasn't enough, other positive effects on the brain were also apparent. The physically fit 18-year-olds were less at risk of getting epilepsy or developing dementia.

I'm not saying cardiovascular fitness when you are 18 has effects stretching decades into the future; it's more likely that someone who is fit at 18 is also more likely to be a fit 30- or 40-year-old, and that it is the fitness in your thirties and forties that affects how well you function and feel at that time of your life. Neither am I saying that physical activity is the only thing that affects IQ, but what I am saying is that it is one factor that works alongside education, nutrition, intellectual stimuli and the genes we are born with. One way to look at this is that we are all born with an IQ-potential. A possible IQ that we can reach. If we are too sedentary, we push ourselves down from that potential. We could do better, so to speak. Regardless of our starting point, we have unused potential if we are too sedentary.

Why is it so difficult for us to understand this?

I spend a lot of time reading scientific papers, but when I come upon this type of research I find it hard to stay interested. It's as if I can't quite absorb it. Perhaps it just seems too good to be true that 15 minutes of play every day can improve reading comprehension and arithmetic in children. And this without the kids even having to read or practise any of the subjects!

If you feel the same way, stick around a while longer and mull over what you've read in this chapter. Think about what it means. Let it sink in, and think about how incredible it is that children's brains not only do better academically but function better overall if they're physically active. The brain's grey and white matter are strengthened in children who move their bodies, just as muscles develop if you lift weights. Isn't it amazing that training can make children and adults *smarter*? It's hard to think of a better reason to encourage kids to put down their tablets and phones and get them to move more – because what parent doesn't want their child to become smarter and have a better working brain?

Have you been taken aback by the findings described in this chapter? I was, too. In fact, I was so surprised that I had to read some of the studies several times over to make sure I had got them right.

We should ask ourselves why no one seems to know about this research. The reason could be spelled out with the letters m-o-n-e-y, as in the case of the effect of physical activity on depression. If a drug or even a dietary supplement had shown this potency, it would have been marketed relentlessly and we all would have heard about it. It's strange, as well as a pity, that not everyone knows that children's – and, for that matter, adults' – brains are influenced this way by exercise. Unlike pharmaceuticals, dietary supplements, computer games and cognitive training methods, physical activities such as playing, walking and running are free of charge. And the body gets a 'twofer' by way of a long list of positive effects that no dietary supplement in the world can match.

THE RIGHT PRESCRIPTION FOR CHILDREN AND TEENAGERS

- For children and adolescents aged 5–17 years, aim for an average of 60 minutes per day of moderate-to-vigorous, mostly aerobic, physical activity. This is in line with the WHO recommendations.
- Elevating the heart rate seems to be especially beneficial for the brain; try to get yours up to around 150bpm.
- It's intensity that counts, not what you do. Physical activity doesn't have to be about working out; play is just as beneficial. As with adults, it isn't *what* children do, it's *that* they do something.
- Shorter bouts of activity count. When children and teenagers move around for 12 minutes, their reading comprehension and ability to focus improve. As little as four minutes of activity at an intensity equal to jogging makes concentration easier. So it's important to get out and play during breaktime, even if it's only for a few minutes!
- Sporadic activity lasting 10–40 minutes at a time leads to temporary improvement in working memory, reading comprehension and attention span.
- Being physically active a few times a week for 2–3 months leads to permanent effects, such as better arithmetic ability, increased creativity and improved executive control (planning, initiative, concentration and impulse control).

CHAPTER 8

HEALTHY AGEING
OF THE BRAIN

*I am physically active, walking, jogging and running for at
least four hours a day. It keeps my body and mind active.*

FAUJA SINGH, AGED 112

I'M SURE WE'VE all seen plenty of examples of how ageing
affects our brain's ability to function. It's not simply about memory;
as we get older, we think more slowly and cognitive functions such
as concentration and multitasking decline. By studying how the
brain works, we've begun to understand why there are differences in
mental abilities between the young and the elderly.

The Stroop test consists of showing the subject a colour word
that is written in a different colour to what the word says – for
example, the word 'blue' spelled out in red letters. The test subject
must quickly identify the colour of the letters that make up the
word – in this case, red – *not* the colour the word says, i.e. blue. Concentration and decision-making are required to suppress the impulse

to choose the colour specified by the word. When the brains of subjects involved in this test are examined, results show that the anterior part of the frontal lobe, the prefrontal cortex, is activated. That is to be expected, since that part of the brain is key to decision-making, focus and impulse control.

Generally, older adults don't perform as well as young people on the Stroop test; they often have trouble resisting the urge to say the word itself, instead of the colour the word is written in, making this an effective test for seeing the differences between the brains of the young and the old.

In young brains, only some parts of the prefrontal cortex are activated during the test, and often only on the left side of the brain. When a 70-year-old performs the test, however, larger parts of the prefrontal cortex are activated, and on both sides of the brain. This probably means that the test requires more mental effort for an older person, and that a larger area of the brain must be pressed into service. It's no different, really, from a young, strapping person being able to lift a chair with one arm, while an older person, who might not be quite as strong, needs to use both arms.

Scientists have named this phenomenon of using both brain halves 'hemispheric symmetry reduction in older adults' (HAROLD). What's interesting is that one segment of 70-year-olds do not exhibit this tendency: those who are physically fit. When they do the test, only one half of their brain lights up, and even fewer areas of the prefrontal cortex are involved; their brains function as if they were younger. Like a muscular 70-year-old who can lift a chair with one arm, a fit older person only needs to use one side of their brain when doing the Stroop test. The test shows that they not only use less of their brain for the task, they also perform above the level of their peers.

THE BRAIN'S AGEING PROCESS CAN BE STOPPED

The HAROLD experiment on 70-year-olds is one of many tests that illustrate that exercise seems to have a remarkable ability to halt the brain's ageing process. As you've read earlier in the book, the hippocampus doesn't shrink but grows in someone who is physically active. The same applies to the frontal lobe – the brain's 'boss', where our most advanced cognitive functions are housed. Like the hippocampus, the frontal lobe shrinks over one's lifespan, which adds to the impairment of our mental capacities. However, physical activity can slow down the shrinkage of the frontal lobe.

The amount by which the frontal lobe shrinks has been linked to how much energy – i.e. how many calories – we expend. In people who move around and use a lot of energy, the frontal lobe seems to dwindle more slowly as they age. The 'thinking' part of their brain is shielded from ageing! By contrast, the frontal lobe of people who don't burn a lot of calories – in other words, those who are very sedentary – shrinks much faster. A few quick runs are not going to make much of a difference, either: we're talking about accumulated calorie expenditure over several years, decades even. We can't achieve this by jogging sporadically around the neighbourhood.

Having a wide pool of test subjects is always a good thing in medical research because it reduces the risk of getting false results. When scientists kept track of about 20,000 women between the ages of 70 and 80 over two decades it became evident that those who exercised regularly retained their memory much longer than those who were sedentary. In addition, focus and attention were sharper in those who were active. The difference was so stark that the brains of the subjects who trained functioned, on average, as if they were three years younger. As is so often the case when it comes to exercise's effects on the brain, we need not make Herculean efforts; a 20-minute daily walk is enough.

THE PILOTS WHO LOST THEIR EDGE

For some individuals, having intact cognitive abilities isn't only essential for normal functioning, it's critical for their work. Gradually losing our ability to focus, multitask and exhibit sound judgement as we age could mean we are no longer able do our job. And there are few professions for which proper cognitive function is as critical as for an airplane pilot.

Healthy ageing in the brain

A team of scientists from Stanford University decided to follow 144 pilots who had to test their flying skills in a simulator on a yearly basis. Their reactions to a series of potentially dangerous situations were observed; scenarios involved engine failure, malfunctioning of the landing gear or the presence of another plane in the wrong airspace that could set the two aircraft on a collision course.

Points were used to grade the pilots' ability to handle these and other types of challenging situations. When they performed the test several years in a row, the results showed that their flying skills gradually became impaired over time. That's no big surprise because the brain ages. However, in one group of pilots their abilities declined twice as fast as other pilots. When the scientists examined that group's genes, they discovered more incidences of a mutation in the gene for BDNF, the brain's fertiliser. In the same group they also noticed that their hippocampus (the memory centre) had shrunk more rapidly compared to the hippocampus of the pilots who did not have that genetic mutation.

The mutation was present in one-third of the pilots; it is estimated that about as many people in the population at large carry this gene. One in three people – us included – have a gene that probably makes their brain age quicker, their hippocampus shrink faster and their mental abilities decline more rapidly.

Is there any way to prevent this? Yes and no. You're born with your genes. It is not possible to change them, so if you happen to carry this gene in its mutated form, well, it's there. However, you can significantly affect how much BDNF your brain makes, and the best way to do this is through physical activity, especially intense exercise like interval training. The scientists who conducted the study made the following statement in an interview: 'There is a clear and proven way to ensure increased BDNF levels in the brain, and that is with physical activity.'

We can also assert that exercise leads to improved circumstances for keeping our intellectual capacities running for longer. We can stop mental and cerebral ageing. For the one-third of us whose genetic make-up has predestined our brain to age a little bit faster, it's imperative to get started on exercise.

Can physical activity improve pilots' flying skills? Personally I would prefer that proper scientific evidence back things up before we draw any definitive conclusions, so at this point my answer is: let's wait and see. But there really is no reason to believe that it can't.

YOU ARE YOUR MEMORY

Of all the cognitive abilities that diminish as we age, memory stands out the most. Having a good memory is so much more than remembering where you put your keys or what was on yesterday's news. Your memory puts everything you do into perspective. Essentially, you are who you are because of your memories. Every decision you make, from the trivial – e.g. the colour of your socks – to your choice of career and where you're going to live, is tied to past experiences.

In every situation we find ourselves in, our memory does a comparison check against past events. Memory anchors us to our lives, and if our ability to remember disappears, we change as individuals. Anyone who has witnessed a person suffering from dementia will know what I'm talking about. As the ability to remember fades, the person becomes a shadow of their former self. Thus, sharpening our memory is something more fundamental than simply increasing the number of words we can recall on a test.

Dementia is unfortunately something that is relevant to all of us. When we reach our 70th birthday, about 2 per cent of us will suffer from dementia. If we are lucky to reach our 90th birthday, almost half of us will. There are between 150,000 and 200,000 people suffering from dementia in Sweden; in the UK it is close to a million, and throughout the world a new case is diagnosed every seven seconds. If this trend continues, there will be 150 million individuals with dementia by 2050. These figures are as grim as the illness itself.

Due to the sheer number of people affected by this disease, pharmaceutical companies have been throwing money at dementia research for a long time; every year several billion dollars are earmarked for the development of dementia drugs. Unfortunately a cure has been elusive, and the result of these expended billions can only be described as weak at best. As of now, there are still no effective medications for dementia.

A drug showing the same promise as a daily walk would be hailed as the most groundbreaking invention since antibiotics.

Walk against dementia

Scientists with far smaller budgets than pharmaceutical companies have investigated whether there's anything that can decrease the risk of dementia, and these scientists have made some incredible discoveries. Not just one but several major studies indicate that a brisk daily walk cuts our risk of developing dementia by 30–40 per cent. The media has not paid enough attention to this, and that's a real shame because it's a mind-boggling statistic.

A drug showing the same promise would become the world's bestselling pharmaceutical in no time, and would probably be hailed as the most groundbreaking invention since antibiotics. The Nobel Prize in physiology and medicine would be in those scientists' pockets. We would all know the drug by name and would probably fight tooth and nail to get it for ourselves and our loved ones to lessen our likelihood of getting dementia. As it is, the thing that has this effect is simply going for a walk, and we don't even have to do it every day – five days a week is plenty.

It isn't only the media that missed this important discovery; a lot of physicians did, too. Many scientists and doctors are focused on other research, such as finding the genes responsible for Alzheimer's, the most common type of dementia. The study of our genes is inarguably thrilling, and of course there is a genetic factor to Alzheimer's, especially if you have close relatives who suffer from it. But for most of us our genetic inheritance is less important than whether or not we are physically active. Research shows unambiguously that it is the sedentary person who needs to worry about dementia – not just those who have a parent or grandparent who has the illness.

Sadly, many people for whom dementia runs in the family believe it doesn't matter if they exercise since they're doomed to develop the disease anyway. This is very unfortunate because it is *especially* important for them to start moving! Most of them can overcome their genetic fate, and more, with regular training.

It's truly mysterious why it has been so difficult to get this message across. It might be that genetic and pharmaceutical research is considered so very high-tech that it fires up our collective imagination and thus makes it more media friendly. The amazing benefit of regular walking is pretty tame in comparison. Our initial reaction is that pharmaceutical money should conjure up a more cutting-edge and innovative cure than a simple walk, but that's not the case. As it happens, walking *is* the best medicine for dementia.

A better world for the brain

How can a walk provide the best protection against dementia? Surely the brain should be exercised with crosswords, Sudokus and different types of brainteaser games? However, research clearly shows that walking is *far* more important than doing the daily crossword, and not just for protecting against dementia but for safeguarding all cognitive abilities. Our brain does not shut off when we walk – far from it; many different mental processes are engaged. Multiple visual impressions need to be synchronised and balanced out, while large areas of the motor cortex are busy coordinating the body's movements. Furthermore, we need to be aware of where we are and where we're going, which presses yet more areas of the brain into service. If we're doing a more complicated activity, such as playing tennis, even more of the brain's systems are called upon. When we compare this to working on a crossword, which mostly involves the language centre, we realise that our mental labour is greater when we move around than when we sit reading a newspaper.

Besides, our brain isn't vacuum-sealed in our cranium; it is covered in what is called the cerebrospinal fluid, a solution filled with nutrients and growth factors that is extremely fine-tuned and hugely influential for how our brain operates. To provide the brain with the best possible conditions in this 'bath', our blood pressure must remain stable. Likewise, blood glucose and blood fats should be in balance. The number of free radicals shouldn't be too high, and the level of inflammation in the body – there is always some level of inflammation in the body – shouldn't be excessive either. Today we know that all these factors are positively impacted when we are physically active, which means the brain is in an ideal environment in anyone who exercises.

The body and the brain are not two separate entities; many of the positive effects that movement has on the body – such as stabilising blood sugar and lowering levels of free radicals – strengthen the brain as well. A strong heart will pump enough blood to provide the brain with the energy it needs. The expression 'a sound mind in a sound body' isn't just a dusty cliché, it's true.

So how active do we need to be to lower our risk of developing dementia? Research has mostly studied walking or light jogging for a total of 150 minutes per week, or half an hour five times a week. Running for 20 minutes three times a week yields comparable results. We're not yet sure what effect weight training has on dementia, so until we know it's better to keep doing what has been proven to work: walking or running.

It isn't only in regards to dementia that movement protects your memory. Getting older impairs memory for most of us, without having anything to do with dementia. The hippocampus shrinks; blood flow to the brain diminishes; there's weaker contact between different areas of the brain. But we can slow these processes down markedly if we stay active. Training slams the brakes on the brain's ageing and improves our memory, whether or not we suffer from dementia.

A picture of healthy ageing

The Canadian star athlete Olga Kotelko died in June 2014 at the age of 95, after an incredibly successful career that included 37 world records and 750 wins. Does her name sound unfamiliar? It's no wonder: Olga didn't begin training at elite levels until she was

77 years old. The long jump and 100m sprint were two of her favourite events, and she became the oldest long jumper in the world after her 90th birthday. Her field of competition narrowed in the final years of her career; in fact, she often didn't have any competitors at all. It was enough for her to turn up at the meet to be given a gold medal.

People who start training and competing in sports when they're over 75 years old are few and far between. This is especially true for those who have never before competed at elite levels. That's why a group of scientists asked Olga if she would allow them to examine her brain under MRI. They were looking to find out if and how the brain is influenced by exercise at such an advanced age. Olga agreed to undergo the MRI and her brain was compared to a group of her peers who had lived like most other 90-year-olds, by resting a lot and harbouring no thoughts of entering athletic competitions. The MRI showed that Olga's brain was healthier, with a larger hippocampus. The white matter in her brain, which transmits information from different parts of the brain, did not show the age-related decline that is normally observed in people in their nineties. And it wasn't just the scans that looked good; Olga's memory was far better than that of her peers.

We can't automatically assume that Olga's brain was in better shape due to her training; it *might* have been different right from the very beginning. However, her level of physical activity is a more plausible explanation for her brain's good health.

Olga's intense training is a perfect example of what scientists call 'successful ageing' of the body and brain. Since Olga started exercising seriously at 77, she demonstrated that, from our brain's perspective, it is never too late to start being physically active. The brain will get stronger no matter how late in life you begin exercising. And you don't need to set your sights on breaking world records or winning medals to obtain results.

Blue zones

There are a few regions in the world where an unusually high percentage of the population reaches the same age as Olga Kotelko – and even older – and who, like her, are untroubled by dementia. These mysterious places, which we call 'blue zones', go against the grain when compared to the rest of the world. There is a blue zone in Sardinia, Italy, another in Okinawa, Japan, another in Costa Rica and one in Småland in southern Sweden!

What is their secret? How can so many people reach 100 years of age and not suffer from dementia? When scientists attempted to find the common denominator between these places, something interesting turned up. To start with, none of the blue zones are in big cities but in small communities or on isolated islands. The people maintain strong social bonds, often with several generations living together. Very few live alone. Additionally, the people in these communities don't stuff themselves with food but follow a stricter diet with fewer calories (but not a starvation diet). Another common factor is that the populations of these blue zones are very active; their exercise tends to be comprised of everyday activities, not hard training.

Scientists don't know which factor (or factors) plays a part in longevity and the absence of dementia in these specific areas; it's probably a combination of all of them. What is fascinating is that people in the blue zones have, on average, lower levels of education, although we know that education is protective against dementia. That physical activity contributes to advanced age is not merely a possibility, then, but very likely. It's also interesting to note that these populations enjoy all the benefits of physical activity – long lives free of dementia – without needing to train hard. It seems their everyday activities keep them from harm – and that is a very good reason for taking a daily walk, always taking the stairs and getting off the bus a stop or two before you reach your destination.

THE RIGHT PRESCRIPTION TO APPLY
THE BRAKES TO THE BRAIN'S AGEING

- All activity matters! Your body takes account of every step, especially when it comes to brain ageing.
- Walk for 20–30 minutes every day, at least five days a week, or run for 20 minutes three times a week. Swimming and cycling are just as good, so long as the level of exertion is the same.
- Weight training is important to stay functional and mobile as we get older. It also seems to have protective effects on the ageing of the brain. However, how *much* protection your brain gets from weight training is still not known. From a brain perspective, I therefore recommend that you prioritise cardiovascular training – here the protective effects on the brain are well known – at least until we know more about the impact of weight training.

CHAPTER 9

A STONE AGE BRAIN IN THE DIGITAL AGE

Nothing in biology makes sense except in the light of evolution.

THEODOSIUS DOBZHANSKY,
EVOLUTIONARY BIOLOGIST

WE'VE SEEN HOW exercise can make you more focused, happier and less anxious and stressed; how training strengthens your memory, makes you more creative and even seems to increase your intelligence. You've discovered the mechanisms that transform running into nothing less than a mental upgrade. Sure, it's easy to be mesmerised by all this research, but personally I believe the most thrilling aspect of it all is not *how* our brain is affected by being physically active, but *why* it happens.

If we want to know how to make our car run smoothly, it is good to understand how it works. The same goes for the brain. If we want to make our brain function better, it's good to start by learning how it works. And we don't need to become neuroscientists or psychiatrists for that. The very best way to make sense of the brain is to see how it has developed. We need to backtrack and look at the history of the brain.

We'll start from the very beginning. Lucy, whose skeleton was found in Ethiopia in the 1970s, is one of our oldest known and preserved human ancestors. She lived approximately 3.2 million years ago, and her brain was about 0.5 litres (nearly 17fl oz) in volume, which is a bit more than one-third of today's average brain volume at 1.3 litres (nearly 44fl oz). If we fast-forward by just over a million years, we'll meet *Homo erectus*, who walked upright and was one step ahead of Lucy and her brain size.* Their brain's volume was just under 1 litre (nearly 34fl oz), and their behaviour had begun to change, too. *Homo erectus* knew how to build a fire and make tools, weapons and clothes.

THE COGNITIVE REVOLUTION

The brain's volume started to increase at a faster pace around 1 million years ago. This could have been due to better nutrition with more protein. Barely 100,000 years ago, our ancestors' intellectual capacity seemed to improve significantly – a phase that is commonly referred to as 'the Cognitive Revolution' – which had significant repercussions. From a historical standpoint, an extremely short period of time saw our ancestors colonise large parts of the globe and go from being a rather inconsequential species among many others in one corner of East Africa, to becoming masters of the earth, without rival at the top of the food chain. On the way they knocked six other human species out of the running (yes, there were at least six other, different species of human in existence). Today, only our species, *Homo sapiens*, is still here. What made us win? We're not entirely sure,

---

* It is far from certain that evolution went from Lucy to *Homo erectus* to *Homo sapiens*. Our ancestors probably existed in parallel with *Homo erectus*.

but it wasn't just having a larger brain. Neanderthals, for example – one of the six species we edged out – had larger brains than ours.

One possibility for our dominance is differences in the cerebral cortex – the outer layer of the brain – which is itself comprised of six distinct layers. The cerebral cortex is the centre of our advanced cognitive functions; mathematical, logical, linguistic and creative thinking abilities can all be found here. This is where the magic happens. In the words of the American astronomer Carl Sagan: 'civilization is a product of the cerebral cortex'.

A larger and more sophisticated cerebral cortex – especially the area situated behind the forehead, in the anterior part of the frontal lobe, the prefrontal cortex – translates into increased cognitive capacity and flexible behaviour. This is a big advantage for survival. We become better hunters, better at defending ourselves against our enemies and, probably most important, more amenable to working together. All this leads to better nutrition with more protein and vitamins, which in turn allows the cerebral cortex to evolve even further. This makes the person smarter and better at surviving and finding food, and so on.

Today our brain looks a bit like long, tightly packed sausages. This structure frees up more room for the cerebral cortex. If the brain were as smooth and polished as a billiard ball, the overall surface area of the cerebral cortex would be smaller, making us considerably more primitive.

THE BRAIN'S MOST IMPORTANT FUNCTION

In principle, only mobile living organisms possess a brain. Plants are not ambulant, so they don't have a brain. It's believed that the first brain cells evolved about 600 million years ago and that their primary task was to coordinate movement in primitive animals. This means the most important function of the first brain cells that emerged on earth was movement. At this point, brain cells did not contribute to sophisticated brain functions like attention, but to simpler reflexes such as moving the organism from place to place in search of food.

The same applies to us humans. Coordination of movements has most likely been our brain's most important function, and it still is. So if the brain's most important task is to get you to move your body, wouldn't it be odd if movement in and of itself were of no importance to the brain?

The body can't move without a brain, and if the body doesn't physically move, the brain can't function as it was meant to.

Did a badly copied gene make us smart?

The human brain is approximately three times the size of that of a chimpanzee, our closest relative. Humans and chimps split from a common ancestor about 6 million years ago, and from what we know today, it seems that the chimp brain has not changed that much since. But during this time the human brain has tripled in size. Moreover, our cerebral cortex has become disproportionately large compared to that of other animals, especially the frontal lobe and its anterior part, the prefrontal cortex.

But what was it that gave our ancestors larger brains and an increasingly sophisticated cerebral cortex, and with those an edge over other species? Many scientists believe the answer can be found in our genes. In 2015, scientists from the Max Planck Institute introduced a gene they believe might have contributed to the fact that you are reading this instead of scouring the savanna trying to find animals to kill.

Genes often have complicated names; this one is called

ARHGAPIIB. It can be found in humans but is missing in related species like the chimpanzee. Interestingly, it looks like this gene came about purely by chance. In one of our ancestors, when a different gene was going to be copied, something went awry, and instead of a whole gene, only a fragment was copied. This fragment, which we call ARHGAPIIB, spurred on the growth of the cerebral cortex.

Our ancestor who by lucky accident was dealt this faulty genetic copy got a slightly larger cerebral cortex, and thus greater cognitive capacity, giving them an advantage in terms of survival. This gene was then passed down to their offspring, whose cerebral cortex grew a bit more, and this is how the brain continued to develop through history.

Perhaps we have chance to thank for our intelligence. If this duplication had not been faulty and created ARHGAPIIB, we might never have made it to the moon, discovered the theory of relativity or painted the Sistine Chapel; instead we would have continued to roam the savanna.

But how do we know it's just this one gene that's behind the expansion of the brain? Our genetic material contains about 23,000 genes, so it could be just about any of them. Well, the answer is that it's impossible to be 100 per cent sure. However, a good indication that ARHGAPIIB could be part of the explanation for this critical evolutionary step came after we implanted the gene in mice, which don't naturally possess ARHGAPIIB, using genetic technology.

Mice have a small cerebral cortex in relation to their body size, and the cortex has no folds; however, something happened to the mice who received ARHGAPIIB. They grew bigger brains, and in several cases their cerebral cortex showed signs of folding. In other words, their brains looked more like ours! The really important question here is, of course, whether the mice became smarter. Scientists don't know the answer to this yet, but are working on it.

THE BIG SWITCH-OVER

No one is oblivious to the fact that over the last few years we've become less active and are spending more time in front of computers and smartphones. This trend is as important as it is troubling, but there are even more interesting trends to be found if we look further back in time. Sometime around 10,000 years ago, our ancestors turned to agriculture after having spent millions of years as hunter-gatherers. The hunter's nomadic lifestyle, with its constant, active search for food, was gradually and over many generations swapped for a lifestyle that required staying more or less in one place. Being a farmer certainly didn't mean you could sit around all day, but it is likely they were less physically active than our hunting ancestors.

The decrease in physical activity that occurred as we went from hunting to agriculture all those years ago is trifling compared to what has happened over the last 200 years, when a really big change has taken place in our activity habits. In just over 200 years we've gone from an agrarian society to an industrialised one – and today a digitalised one – where most of us do not need to go out and actively gather food.

What was the most important daily task for most of humanity's history has become something most of us don't have to worry about any more, never mind be physically active to succeed at. Today all our food is available at the supermarket, and even online, where we can have it delivered to our door to avoid having to move at all.

Half as many steps

These changes have had an enormous impact on our activity levels. We are far less physically active than in any point of our history, but *how much* less? It's difficult to pinpoint the number exactly, since our ancestors did not have access to pedometers, but by examining the activity patterns of people who still live as hunter-gatherers and comparing those to farmers, it's possible to make an educated guess.

The Hadza people live in north Tanzania. The tribe has about 1,000 members, about half of whom live as hunter-gatherers. They have no domestic animals, they don't cultivate the earth and they don't have permanent settlements. Instead they subsist by hunting and building temporary shelters for the night. Their language is probably one of the oldest spoken languages on earth. Basically, the Hadza live the same way their – and our – ancestors lived 10,000 years ago. They are among the very last people on the planet who live as hunter-gatherers, and as such they give important clues to our ancestors' way of life.

So, how active are they? When members of the tribe were kitted out with pedometers, they showed that the men walked an average of 8–10km (5–6.2 miles) a day, the equivalent of 16,000–18,000 steps, while the women took slightly fewer steps on average. This is about how much we believe our hunter-gatherer ancestors walked.

And what about the farmers? To get some clues, we can observe Amish people in the US, who live in an agrarian society pretty much like we did 200 years ago. The Amish have chosen to forgo all modern amenities and don't watch TV, aren't connected to the Internet and don't use electricity. They move considerably more than we do. The men walk about 18,000 steps a day, while the women, like Hadza women, take slightly fewer steps. Now compare this to the 5,000–6,000 steps that Americans and Europeans walk daily on average and you'll realise that the Hadza and the Amish walk about three times as much as today's population in Europe and the US. It is likely that we've cut our level of activity by up to two-thirds during our transition from a hunter-gatherer society to today's modern civilisation.

In a blink of an eye

The 10,000 years that have gone by since we made the switch to an agrarian society might seem like an eternity. However, from a biological perspective this is a very short period. Our time as farmers makes up only *1 per cent* of the history of humankind. The approximately 200 years that have passed since the beginning of industrialisation can also feel like a stretch since the 1800s are undeniably long past, but from an evolutionary standpoint it is just the blink of an eye.

If we condense the history of humanity into a period of 24 hours, we can see that we were hunter-gatherers until 11.40pm. We didn't become industrialised until 11.59.40pm, 20 seconds before midnight. We entered the digital age, i.e. connected to the Internet, at 11.59.59pm – one second before midnight!

If we consider the time it normally takes for species to develop, it's obvious that evolution happens over a very long time. It takes tens of thousand years, and often longer, before major changes occur within a species. That goes for humans too. We have not changed in any major way during the last 10,000 years. Today's people are close to genetically identical to those who lived 100, 1,000 and even 10,000 years ago. If a child was born 10,000 years ago and then brought up in our world, we wouldn't notice anything different about him or her.

We're walking out of step with our biological age, or should I say we're *sitting* out of step.

Think about it: over a period that is basically a blip in our history, we've made gigantic changes to our lifestyle that have cut our need for physical activity by 60–70 per cent. If we compare that to evolution's development of humanity as a species – which, again, happens very slowly – you can see that our lifestyle changes have far outpaced the evolution of our bodies and brains. Evolution is lagging behind. Biologically, our bodies and brains are still on the savanna and we're more hunter-gatherers than farmers. Add this to what you've read in this book so far – that your brain is strengthened by exercise, that physical activity makes you happier and less stressed, that it makes you more creative and focused, that a lack of it can lead you to feel anxious, sad and unfocused – and it's easy to conclude that many of today's common psychological problems stem from our lack of physical activity. We're walking out of step with our biological age, or should I say we're *sitting* out of step.

Why are we lazy if it's so beneficial to be active?

There is absolutely no doubt that our bodies and brains have evolved to handle activity levels far greater than those we engage in today. The paradox is that we are lazy. If it's so good for us to go outside for a walk or a run, why is it so nice just to lounge on the sofa and snack on crisps? Why is the brain avoiding doing something so good as exercise? Because throughout most of human history we've had to deal with an energy and calorie deficit – not an excess, like today. Calorie-dense meals were rare for our hunting ancestors, and it was always better to eat food right away lest someone else tried to steal it from you. That's why calorie-rich foods taste so good: your brain wants you to eat all of them to fill up your energy stores.

When our ancestors on the savanna came upon a tree full of sweet, calorific fruits, it wasn't particularly smart to pick one and save the rest for later, as we have been taught to do nowadays when we're offered a piece of chocolate from a box. For them, a better strategy was to eat it all immediately so as not to miss out on all those precious calories. If they waited until the next day, the fruits would probably all be gone; someone else would have taken them. However, that urge is still with us, so when we're faced with a box of chocolates, our brain says: *Scarf down the entire box right now! Eat every little bit, otherwise someone else will snag them! We might need the calories tomorrow if there's no food.* That's why we feel compelled to eat the whole box.

The body's energy reserves don't just depend on how much you fill them from eating, but also on how much energy you expend. Not using up energy unnecessarily, and being able to keep a little in reserve around the middle in case of famine, has been a survival trump card for us humans. We have an inner urge to economise our efforts and to conserve energy that can tide us over when times are hard. So when you're lounging on the sofa in front of the TV, dreaming up excuses to cancel that run or walk, it is, paradoxically, your hunter-gatherer brain that is telling you to stay put: *Sit and save energy. It'll come in handy when there's no food and you need energy.* By keeping you on the sofa, wolfing down potato chips, your body and your brain are basically preparing you for a future period of starvation – only, that period never comes in today's world.

It's obvious that this inherent urge to save calories has consequences for our weight. If you're not convinced, look at what happens in places that were once considered Third World countries and that have since experienced rapid economic growth, giving themselves over in a few short decades to a lifestyle full of fast food, ever-present sugar and couch-potato TV watching. Rates of obesity have skyrocketed in these countries. It is well known that this new lifestyle leads us to gain weight, but we are not as familiar with the consequences for our brain.

FULL SPEED BACKWARDS!

Huge technological advancements over the last decades have given us commodities such as the Internet, smartphones and food that can be ordered from home at the click of a button. Meanwhile, we're moving further and further from the life we evolved for. Our increased comfort makes us restless, anxious and unhappy. Again, *why* do our mental functions suffer when we're sedentary and why are they boosted when we exercise?

Here, too, the answer can be found in the past. Basically, our brain works the same as our ancestors' did 10,000 years ago. They didn't compete in marathons or work out to get in shape before swimsuit season. They were physically active in order to survive: they ran or walked in search of food, to get away from danger and to find new places to live.

The brain is hard-wired to give us a kick of dopamine so that we feel better when we move our body, since hunting, running away from danger and finding new places to settle down increase our chances of survival. Since the brain hasn't changed in 10,000 years, the same mechanism is active within us today, so when we engage in behaviours that increased our ancestors' chances of survival, our brain rewards us with a feeling of pleasure to encourage us to repeat those behaviours.

When you come home after your run or walk, your brain interprets the activity as you having been out to look for food or a better place to live, and you'll be rewarded with a feeling of wellbeing. You are not feeling the positive effects of dopamine, serotonin and endorphins because you've read in a health magazine that it's good for you to exercise; you are getting the reward because your brain thinks you've increased your chances of survival. That's also how we're able to understand why we are 'punished' by feeling lousy when we're sedentary. You don't catch any food by remaining seated all day, and this doesn't lead you to find a new home either. Being sedentary has never been good for our survival, which is why it makes many of us feel sick to this day.

In this light, it's easier to understand why physical activity strengthens other cerebral functions. When our ancestors hunted for food, it was important that they stayed focused. If you sneak up on an animal on the savanna, you need to concentrate and react to the smallest movement to boost your odds of making the kill. That's probably why you and I become more focused when we move our bodies.

Exercise improves memory, but why is that? We don't need to improve our memory when we go for a run; we need it when we study for an exam or read a report. The reason is probably that movement means we see new places and new environments. Being sedentary and staying rooted in one spot makes the brain think we aren't experiencing or seeing anything new. Our brain has not evolved for us to experience new things through a smartphone or a computer; it thinks that sitting still means we are not experiencing new sensory stimuli and therefore we don't need memory to store the stimuli that are not there.

The brain is still on the savanna

Your brain doesn't care that the world no longer looks like what it has evolved for. It's still very much on the savanna, and it will work a bit better if you treat it as if it were. Exercising less is, of course, not the only change in our lifestyle and environment that has affected our brain's performance and how we feel. Environmental toxins, urbanisation, modern diets and completely different social structures also play an enormous role. Still, lack of physical activity is one of the most important changes with regards to our physical and mental health, and our decreasing level of exercise is a problem that can be solved quite simply. While we may not be able to ditch our lives in the city and move into the woods to hunt, we can move our bodies a little more. We can take a major step towards the life our brain has evolved for by becoming more active – for which our brains will offer us ample rewards.

Many of us feel that something is amiss even though we live in unprecedented material comfort. But it's not that strange that we feel this way, because our modern society has removed us from the life we were built for. The lifestyle changes we have experienced over just a few generations have brought about incredible advantages – just keep in mind how much our lifespan has increased. On the other hand, we tend to become depressed, anxious, stressed and unfocused for the simple reason that our brain has not evolved to deal with our current way of life.

You can relieve a great deal of this malaise by engaging in more exercise. Of course, this doesn't mean all mental problems can be solved by running. But what it does mean is that if we feel low or are stressed out, maybe we should ask ourselves whether there's anything in our way of life that could be altered and not automatically assume that all problems can be cured by taking a pill.

'Walking is man's best medicine.'

If I were reading this book, I would be thinking by now that if exercise was truly that good for the brain, then everyone would be aware of it, right? Surely this should be as widely known as the fact that smoking is bad for you and that coffee wakes you up. I believe we've always known how good physical activity is for the brain, but over the past 150 years we've forgotten. 'Walking is man's best medicine.' These words are not a cliché from a health magazine – they came from the mouth of Hippocrates, the father of medicine, who as far back as 2,500 years ago, and without the benefit of modern medical technology, understood how important moving our body was for our physical and mental health.

In the last 150 years, we've experienced staggering medical advances that have given us everything from vaccines to antibiotics, MRI scans to molecular-targeting cancer drugs. In the wake of all these amazing discoveries – and they truly are amazing – everything that was obvious to us earlier seems to have fallen by the wayside.

We've forgotten that the body and the brain's most important medicine might be bodily movement. Hopefully this lack of awareness will change. Lately, research has caught up with and confirmed Hippocrates' historic yet wise words. We haven't quite grasped just *how* important movement is and which mechanisms are responsible for turning a run into a mental upgrade, but it's as if history were coming back to us, because one of our most sophisticated medical technologies – the MRI – has made us revisit the worth of our least sophisticated medicine, physical activity.

Being physically active isn't about being a jock or having six-pack abs; it's about providing the brain with the most advantageous conditions so that it can perform at its best.

THE MIND-BODY METHOD

It's not about being a jock

Thanks to present-day mega-health hype, and because every other magazine on newsstands is about fitness, tickets to many major marathons sell out within hours. At the same time, many people feel that they don't want to or can't take part in this exercise hysteria. I have every sympathy for those who feel like that, and my advice is to forget about long-distance running. Forget about the fitness profiles on Instagram. Forget about the health magazines. But make sure you do some sort of exercise.

Being physically active isn't about being a jock or having six-pack abs; it's about providing the brain with the most advantageous conditions so that it can perform at its best. Brain exercise apps have become a multibillion-dollar industry. Forget about them – they don't work. Also, be very cautious of expensive nutritional supplements and other 'miracle methods' that are supposed to work wonders for the brain – they're ineffective as well. Instead, spend time on what science has so clearly shown works to strengthen your brain: moving your body. It's free. And it's not important *what* you do or *where* you do it; what counts is *that* you do something. It will have some immediate effects on your wellbeing and your mental faculties, but you will really notice it after you have worked out regularly over a longer period.

No one would be happier than me if hanging out on the sofa, eating crisps and binge-watching TV was the best we could do for our brain's health. And it would be awesome if there were cognitive training methods and nutritional supplements that made us feel alert, happy and focused all the time. Sadly, research clearly shows that this is far from reality. Our brains have evolved for physical activity, and they will perform much better if we move our bodies!

CHAPTER 10

THE RIGHT PRESCRIPTION FOR THE BRAIN

*Yes, science is, in a sense, 'reducing' us to the physiological processes of a
not-very-attractive three-pound organ. But what an organ!*

STEVE PINKNER, professor in psychology, Harvard

WE'VE COME TO the most important part of the book, which I
have left for last. After looking at all the research on how exercise
affects the brain, what is the most beneficial activity level for the
brain? How do we exercise to achieve maximum results? It is actually
difficult to give an exact answer to that question but we can draw a
few conclusions based on all the studies that have been done:

- Most important: the brain counts every step! Five minutes
  of walking is better that nothing. It's obviously better to
  walk for 30 minutes than five minutes, but five minutes will
  count, too. Do something you enjoy!
- If you want to get the maximum effect for your brain from
  exercise, run for 45 minutes at least three times a week. You

get the same positive effects if you play soccer, bicycle, swim, cross-country ski or do anything else that raises the pulse. However, doing more than this won't lead to any additional positive effects for the brain; it will only increase your cardiovascular fitness.

- Don't think of the three sessions of 45 minutes in terms of 'I'll either do this or do nothing.' The most important thing is that you do *something*. If you go from doing no exercise to a doing a little, such as walking to work, you will see great effects.

- Focus on cardiovascular training. Weight training does have positive effects on the brain, but aerobic training is better. So if you like lifting weights, don't forget to include an endurance segment.

- Interval training is good exercise but less so from the brain's standpoint, because you become so tired that the immediate after-effects are less beneficial. You won't be more creative in the hours after interval training, whereas you will after less strenuous training such as running at a normal pace. That being said, interval training and other strenuous exercise are no doubt good for the brain over the long term because intense effort strongly increases levels of BDNF.

- Keep at it, keep at it, keep at it! The structural changes that come from redrawing the brain's architecture take time. An occasional run or walk will instantly provide better blood flow to the brain, but it takes time to create new brain cells and new blood vessels and to strengthen the connections between different areas of the brain – months or perhaps even longer. Those who train regularly a few times a week for six months will notice the biggest change.

AFTERWORD

INSIDE YOUR CRANIUM you have the most complex structure in the universe. An organ that is constantly active, from the day you're born until you draw your last breath. An organ that is you. Because you *are* your brain. So why did I write a book about how the brain is affected by physical activity? Because modern neuroscience has shown that maybe the most important thing we can do for our brain – and therefore ourselves – is to be physically active. If this is not a story worth telling, what is?

However, writing a science book for a general readership about how the human brain is affected by bodily movement is a challenge. After all, what we're attempting to describe is an organ so enormously complex that we may never fully understand all its inner workings. Currently, neuroscience is advancing at the speed of light. Every year about 100,000 scientific studies are published about the brain – that's one study every four minutes, 24/7, year round. Our knowledge increases, literally, by the hour. Despite this, we've barely begun to scratch the surface.

It took scientists 40 years to map the brain activities of the small roundworm (*Caenorhabditis elegans*), one of the animals that has been used most frequently in basic brain research. That is, if it's even correct to call what it has a brain, since the tiny worm possesses only about 300 brain cells with a total of 800 connections between them. Compare that to the human brain's 86 billion cells with more than 86 trillion (86,000 billion) connections.

In other words, there's still a staggering amount we don't know about how the brain works, not least of which is how it is affected by exercise. In this book I've attempted to go over the picture that neuroscience presents us at this moment. No doubt future studies will reveal many new, as yet unknown mechanisms by which physical activity strengthens the brain. However, I'm not in the least worried that this book's main message won't still be current in 10 or even 50 years' time. The benefits of exercise for your brain are *enormous*!

Neuroscience isn't just a way to find causes and treatments for brain diseases; it also helps us to understand ourselves. Occasionally research has managed to confirm things that seem obvious – like how important it is for us to socialise with others, or that alcohol breaks down the brain – but sometimes the discoveries have been surprising. We don't need studies to tell us that we feel good from being physically active, but it may not be quite so obvious that exercise has such a big effect on our cognitive abilities (including creativity, stress tolerance, focus and even intelligence) and that it might be one of the most important things we can do.

This book is not about my opinions or hopes but about the science that shows what *is*. At the same time, it's important for me to emphasise that this is not a scientific report but a book on science aimed at a general audience. As such, I've had to simplify certain concepts to make the book more readable and interesting. I've included a list of references for the research this book is based on, so if you want to dig deeper and get a more complete picture of how physical activity affects the brain, you can go to the sources and find out even more. But before you do that, put down this book, get out there and move – exercise your brain!

GLOSSARY

AMYGDALA An almond-sized area of the brain that controls feelings of fear and emotional reactions. There are two amygdalae, one on each side of the brain. The amygdala belongs to the 'reptilian brain' – the primitive part of the brain that has remained with us throughout evolution. It is responsible for quickly putting the body on alert: fight or flight!

AXON A tendril-like offshoot from a brain cell that passes signals between the cells.

BDNF (brain-derived neurotrophic factor) A protein created by the brain that has been shown to be important for many brain functions, like creating new brain cells, as well as for memory and general wellbeing.

CEREBELLUM Situated at the back of the skull, this part of the brain is important for motor control and balance. The cerebellum makes up 10 per cent of the brain's total volume.

CEREBRAL CORTEX The brain's outer layer and its most sophisticated part, it is also the part of the brain where 'major work' is carried out. It consists mainly of cell bodies and is, unlike the rest of the brain, made up of six layers.

CORTISOL A stress hormone produced by the adrenal glands (situated on top of the kidneys) that mobilises energy and increases heart rate and blood pressure and prepares us for fight or flight. Long-term high cortisol levels have negative effects for the brain, especially the hippocampus.

DOPAMINE A substance that transmits signals between brain cells and is important for wellbeing and, in particular, motivation, 'drive' and reward. It is also important for concentration and movement.

ENDOCANNABINOIDS Endogenous substances that can produce pain relief and euphoria. They have receptors in common with marijuana and tetrahydrocannbinol (THC/cannabis).

ENDORPHINS Endogenous morphine (i.e. morphine that originates within the body). A group of hormones created in the brain (and the rest of the body) that can provide pain relief and euphoria.

EXECUTIVE FUNCTIONS or **COGNITIVE FUNCTIONS** A collective term for functions such as impulse control and concentration, and the ability to change and adapt behaviour to current surroundings.

FRONTAL LOBE The anterior part of the brain. Logical and abstract thinking, as well as emotional control, are situated here. The frontal lobe is the most advanced part of the brain.

GABA (gamma-aminobutyric acid) A neurotransmitter (a molecule that sends signals between brain cells) that calms the brain's activity.

GREY MATTER This is mainly composed of neuronal cell bodies. The grey colour isn't noticeable until after death; a living brain is more pink in colour.

HIPPOCAMPUS Part of the brain that is as big as a thumb. There is one hippocampus on each side of the brain. The hippocampus is important for memory, emotional control and spatial orientation. It is the part of the brain that is probably most affected by physical activity.

HPA AXIS (hypothalamic–pituitary–adrenal axis) The brain's most important stress control mechanism. It starts in the hypothalamus, which sends a signal to the pituitary gland, which in turn signals the adrenal glands to produce the stress hormone cortisol.

HYPOTHALAMUS A central area in the brain important for blood pressure, heart rate, body temperature and metabolism.

MRI (magnetic resonance imaging) A sophisticated medical imaging technique that displays body organs in high resolution. Functional MRI is used to observe different areas of the brain as they are activated, which is done by measuring blood flow to the different areas. Significant blood flow indicates high activity in the area. An MRI machine is the size of a car, and the patient is pushed into a tube that looks like a small tunnel. A magnetic field is created in the tunnel that is so strong that the magnet that creates the field must be chilled in liquid nitrogen at a temperature of −200°C.

NEUROGENESIS The process of creating new brain cells. It used to be believed that new brain cells were only created in children, but now we know that new brain cells are also created through adult life.

NEURON A brain cell.

NORADRENALINE A substance in the brain that controls alertness and concentration, among other things (also known as norepinephrine).

NUCLEUS ACCUMBENS A small part of the brain that is important for our reward system and for controlling our behaviour. Dopamine is an important part of the nucleus accumbens, and we feel good when the levels of dopamine rise in that area.

PET SCAN (positron emission tomography) A sophisticated medical imaging technique whereby radioactive substances are injected into the body. It is used for research and in healthcare to locate tumours, among other things.

PITUITARY A pea-sized gland in the brain that regulates several of the body's important hormones, like the stress hormone cortisol. The 'p' in pituitary is the 'P' in the HPA axis.

PREFRONTAL CORTEX The anterior part of the frontal lobe. The seat of our most sophisticated intellectual functions, like anticipating the future, adapting or conforming to changes, putting off rewards, and acting towards others.

REPTILIAN BRAIN Part of the brain that has been preserved through evolution and that we have in common with simpler mammals. Functions like fight or flight are located here. The reptilian brain makes us *react to* danger but does not *anticipate* it. However, the reptilian brain is more of a metaphor; it isn't as simple as believing we have an inner reptile wrapped in a layer of advanced cognition.

SEROTONIN A substance in the brain that is vital for our mood, especially for calm and inner strength.

SSRI (selective serotonin reuptake inhibitor) The most common pharmaceutical used in treating depressive disorders. It acts by increasing levels of the neurotransmitter serotonin in the brain, but it also affects noradrenaline and dopamine.

SYNAPSE The small space between two brain cells where the contact between cells happens. The cells don't touch but send signal substances such as dopamine, serotonin and GABA to each other.

TEMPORAL LOBE The part of the brain located behind the temple. It is important for memory, among other things.

THALAMUS A central part of the brain that a lot of information passes through. It functions at times like a filter to make sure we're not overloaded with information.

WHITE MATTER The connections between brain cells. They are situated beneath the grey matter and consist of long, tendril-like axons. The white colour comes from the fatty substance called myelin that coats the axons and increases the speed of signal transmission.

BIBLIOGRAPHY

1. Your Changeable Brain

Lunghi, C. et al. 'A cycling lane for brain rewiring.' *Current Biology* (2015). DOI:10.1016/j.cub.2015.10.026.

Smith, S. et al. 'A positive-negative mood of population covariation links brain connectivity, demographics and behavior.' *Nature Neuroscience* 18 (2015): 565–7.

Voss, M. et al. 'Plasticity of brain networks in a randomized intervention trial of exercise training in older adults.' *Frontiers in Aging Neuroscience* (2010). DOI:10.3389/fnagi.2010.00032.

2. Run Away from Stress

Agudelo, L. et al. 'Skeletal muscle PGC-1a1 modulates kynurenine metabolism and mediates resilience to stress-induced depression.' *Cell* (2014).

American Psychological Association. *Stress in America: Paying with our health.* (2015). Available at: https://www.apa.org/news/press/releases/stress/2014/financial-stress.

Bonhauser, M. et al. 'Improving physical fitness and emotional well-being in adolescents of low socioeconomic status in Chile: results of a school-based controlled trial.' *Health Promotion International* (2005). DOI:10.1093/heapro/dah603.

Colcombe, S.J., Erickson, K.I., Scalf, P.E. et al. 'Aerobic exercise training increases brain volume in aging humans.' *The Journals of Gerontology. Series A, Biological Sciences and Medical Sciences* 61 (2006): 1166–70.

Dishman, R. et al. 'Increased open field locomotor and striatal GABA binding after activity wheel running.' *Physiology & Behavior* 60; 3 (1996): 699–705.

Erickson, K.I. et al. 'Physical activity, fitness, and gray matter volume.' *Neurobiology of Aging* (2014). DOI:10.1016/j.neurobiolaging.2014.03.034.

Feinstein, J. 'The human amygdala and the induction and experience of fear.' *Current Biology* (2011). DOI:http//dx.doi.org/10.1016/j.cub.2010.11.042.

Hassmen, P. et al. 'Physical exercise and psychological well-being: a population study in Finland.' *Preventive Medicine* 30; 1 (2000): 17–25.

Kim, M. et al. 'The structural integrity of an amygdala-prefrontal lobe pathway predicts trait anxiety.' *Journal of Neuroscience* 29; 37 (2009): 11614–18.

Monk, S. et al. 'Amygdala and ventrolateral prefrontal cortex activation to masked angry faces in children and adocescents with generalized anxiety disorder.' *Archives of General Psychiatry* (2008). DOI: 101001/archpsyc.65.5.568.

Ströhe, A. et al. 'The acute antipanic and anxiolytic activity of aerobic exercise in patients with panic disorder and healthy control subjects.' *Journal of Psychiatric Research* 43 (2009): 1013–1017.

Trom, D. et al. 'Reduced structural connectivity of a major frontolimbic pathway in generalized anxiety disorder.' *Archives of General Psychiatry* 69; 9 (2012): 925–34.

Zschucke, E. et al. 'The stress-buffering effect of acute exercise: evidence for HPA axis negative feedback.' *Psychoneuroendocrinology* 51 (2015): 414–25.

3. Improved Concentration

Beak, D. et al. 'Effect on treadmill exercise on social interaction and tyrosine hydroxylase expression in the attention-deficit/hyperactivity disorder rat.' *Journal of Exercise Rehabilitation* (2014).

Bubl, A. et al. 'Elevated background noise in adult attention deficit hyperactivity disorder is associated with inattention.' *PLoS One* (2015). DOI:10.1371/journal.pone.0118271.

Colcombre, S. et al. 'Cardiovascular fitness, cortical plasticity, and aging.' *PNAS* (2004).

Eun Sang J. et al. 'Duration-dependence of the effect of treadmill exercise on hyperactivity in attention deficit hyperactivity disorder rats.' *Journal of Exercise Rehabilitation* 10; 2 (2014): 75– 80.

Hillman, C. et al. 'Effects of the FIT Kids randomized controlled trial on executive control and brain function.' *Pediatrics* 134 (2014): e1063–71.

Hoang, T. et al. 'Effect of early adult patterns of physical activity and television viewing on midlife cognitive function.' *JAMA Psychiatry* (2015). DOI:10.1001/jamapsychiatry.2015.2468.

Hoza, B. et al. 'A randomized trial examining the effects of aerobic physical activity on attention deficit/hyperactivity disorder symptoms in young children.' *Journal of Abnormal Child Psychology* 43 (2015): 655–77.

Silva, A. et al. 'Measurement of the effect of physical exercise on the concentration of individuals with ADHD.' *PLoS One* (2015). DOI:10.1371/journal.pone.0122119.

Smith, A. et al. 'Pilot physical activity intervention reduces severity of ADHD symptoms in young children.' *Journal of Attention Disorders* 17; 1 (2013): 70–82.

Volkow, N. et al. 'Evaluating dopamine reward pathway in ADHD.' *JAMA* 302; 10 (2009): 1084–1.

4. The Real Happy Pill

Arai, Y. et al. 'Self-Reported Exercise Frequency and Personality: A Population-Based Study in Japan.' *Perceptual and Motor Skills* 87 (1998): 1371–5.

Blumenthal, J. et al. 'Effects of exercise training on older patients with major depression.' *Archives of Internal Medicine* 159; 19 (1999): 2349–56.

Dwivedi, Y. et al. 'Altered gene expression of brain-derived neurotrophic factor and receptor tyrosine kinase B in postmortem brain of suicide subjects.' *Archives of General Psychiatry* 60 (2003): 804–15.

Fernandes, M.F.A. et al. 'Leptin suppresses the rewarding effects of running via STAT3 signaling in dopamine neurons.' *Cell Metabolism* (2015).

Gustafsson, et al. 'The acute response of plasma brain-derived neurotrophic factor as a result of exercise in major depressive disorder.' *Psychiatry Research* 169; 3 (2009): 244–8.

Hassmén, P. et al. 'Physical exercise and psychological well-being.' *Prev. Med.* (2000). DOI: 10.1006/pmed.1999.0597.

Lang, U. et al. 'BDNF serum concentration in healthy volunteers are associated with depression-related personality traits.' *Neuropsychopharmacology* 29 (2004): 795–8.

Mammen, G. et al. 'Physical activity and the prevention of depression: a systematic review of prospective studies.' *American Journal of Preventive Medicine* 45; 5 (2013): 649–57.

Numakawa, T. et al. 'The role of brain-derived neurotrophic factor in comorbid depression: Possible linkage with steroid hormones, cytokines, and nutrition.' *Frontiers in Psychiatry* (2014). DOI:10.3389/fpsyt.2014.00136.

Potgeiter, J.R. et al. 'Relationship between adherence to exercise and scores on extraversion and neuroticism.' *Perceptual and Motor Skills* 81 (1998): 520–2.

Rothman, S. et al. 'Activity dependant, stress-responsive BDNF-signaling and the quest for optimal brain health and resilience throughout the lifespan.' *Neuroscience* 239 (2013): 228–40.

5. Jog Your Memory

Bartol, T. et al. 'Nanoconnectomic upper bound on the variability of synaptic plasticity.' *Neuroscience* (2016). DOI:10.7554/eLife.10778.

Chapman, S. et al. 'Shorter term aerobic exercise improves brain, cognition, and cardiovascular fitness in aging.' *Frontiers in Aging Neuroscience* (2013). DOI:10.3389/fnagi.2013.00075.

Ericson, K. et al. 'Exercise training increases size of hippocampus and improves memory.' *PNAS* (2010). DOI: 10.1073/pnas.1015950108.

Eriksson, P. et al. 'Neurogenesis in the adult human hippocampus.' *Nature Medicine* 4 (1998): 1313–17.

Fastenrath, M. et al. 'Dynamic modulation of amygdala-hippocampal connectivity by emotional arousal.' *The Journal of Neuroscience* 34; 42 (2014): 13935–47.

Kohman, R. et al. 'Voluntary wheel running reverses age-induced changes in hippocampal gene expression.' *PLoS One* (2011). DOI:10.1371/journal.pone.0022654.

Leraci, A. et al. 'Physical exercise and acute restraint stress differentially modulate hippocampal BDNF transcripts and epigenic mechanism in mice.' *Hippocampus* (2015). DOI:10.1002/hip.22458.

O'Keefe, J. 'Place units in the hippocampus of the freely moving rat.' *Experimental Neurology* 51 (1976): 78–109.

Pereira, A. et al. 'An in vivo correlate of exercise-induced neurogenesis in the adult dentate gyrus.' *PNAS* (2007). DOI:10.1073pnas.0611721104.

Rhodes, J. et al. 'Neurobiology of mice selected for high voluntary wheel-running activity.' *Integrative and Comparative Biology* 45 (2005): 438–55.

Roig, M. et al. 'A single bout of exercise improves motor memory.' *PLoS One* (2012). DOI:10.1371/journal.pone.0044594.

Schmidt-Kassow, M. et al. 'Physical exercise during encoding improves vocabulary learning in young female adults: a neuroendocrinological study.' *PLoS One* 8; 5 (2013): e64172.

Smith, C. 'Medial temporal lobe activity during retrieval of semantic memory is related to the age of the memory.' *Journal of Neuroscience* (2009). DOI:10.1523/JNEUROSCI.4545-08.2009.

Winter, B. et al. 'High impact running improves learning.' *Neurobiology of Learning and Memory* (2007). DOI:10.1016/j.nlm.2006.11.003.

6. Train Yourself Creative

Colzato, L. et al. 'The impact of physical exercise on convergent and divergent thinking.' *Frontiers in Human Neuroscience* (2013). DOI:10.3389/fnhum.2013.00824.

Oppezzo, M. et al. 'Give your ideas some legs: the positive effect of walking on creative thinking.' *Journal of Experimental Psychology: Learning, Memory, and Cognition* 40; 4 (2014): 1142–52.

Steinberg, H. et al. 'Exercise enhances creativity independently of mood.' *British Journal of Sports Medicine* 31 (1997): 240–5.

7. The Growing Brain

Burzynska, A. et al. 'Physical activity and cardiorespiratory fitness are beneficial for white matter in low-fit older adults.' *PLoS One* (2014). DOI: 10.1371/journal.pone.0107413.

Castelli, D. et al. 'Physical fitness and academic achievement in third- and fifth-grade students.' *Journal of Sport and Exercise Psychology* 29; 2 (2007): 239–52.

Chaddock, C. et al. 'A neuroimaging investigation of the association between aerobic fitness, hippocampal volume, and memory performance in preadolescent children.' *Brain Research* 1358 (2010): 172–83.

Chaddock-Hayman, L. et al. 'Aerobic fitness is associated with greater white matter integrity in children.' *Frontiers in Human Neuroscience* (2014). DOI:10.3389/fnhum.2014.00584.

Davis, C.L. et al. 'Exercise improves executive function and achievement and alters brain activation in overweight children: a randomized, controlled trial.' *Health Psychology* 30; 1 (2011): 91–8.

Hillman, C. et al. 'The effect of acute treadmill walking on cognitive control and academic achievement in preadolescent children.' *Neuroscience* 159; 3 (2009): 1044–54.

Ma, J. et al. 'Four minutes of in-class high-intensity interval activity improves selective attention in 9- to 11-year olds.' *Applied Physiology Nutrition and Metabolism* (2015). DOI:10.1139/apnm-2014-0309.

Martikainen, S. et al. 'Higher levels of physical activity are associated with lower hypothalamic-pituitary-adrenocortical axis reactivity to psychosocial stress in children.' *Journal of Clinical Endocrinology and Metabolism* (2012). DOI:101210/jc.2012-3745.

Metha, R. et al. 'Standing up for learning: a pilot investigation on the neurocognitive benefits of stand-biased school desks.' *International Journal of Environmental Research and Public Health* (2015). DOI:10.3390/ijerph 13010059.

Nyberg, J. et al. 'Cardiovascular fitness and later risk of epilepsy: a Swedish population-based cohort study.' *Neurology* 81; 12 (2013): 1051–7.

Raine, L. et al. 'The influence of childhood aerobic fitness on learning and memory.' *PLoS One* (2013). DOI:10.1371/journal.pone.0072666.

Rasberry, C. et al. 'The association between school-based physical activity, including physical education, and academic performance: a systematic review of the literature.' *Preventive Medicine* 52; Suppl 1 (2011): S10–20. DOI:10.1016/j.ypmed.2011.01.027.

Rauner, R. et al. 'Evidence that aerobic fitness is more salient than weight status in predicting standardized math and reading outcomes in fourth-through eighth-grade students.' *Pediatrics* (2013). DOI:10.1016/j.jpeds.2013.01.006.

Tine, M. et al. 'Acute aerobic exercise: an intervention for the selective visual attention and reading comprehension of low-income adolescents.' *Frontiers in Psychology* (2014). DOI:10.3389/fpsyg.2014.00575.

van Eimeren, L. et al. 'White matter microstructures underlying mathematical abilities in children.' *NeuroReport* (2008). DOI:10.1097/WNR.obo13e32 8307f5c1.

Åberg, M. et al. 'Cardiovascular fitness is associated with cognition in young adulthood.' *PNAS USA*. 106; 49 (2009): 20906–11.

8. Healthy Ageing in the Brain

Colcombe, S. et al. 'Aerobic exercise training increases brain volume in aging humans.' *The Journals of Gerontology: Series A, Biological Sciences and Medical Sciences* 61 (2006): 1166–70.

Hyodo, K. et al. 'The association between aerobic fitness and cognitive function in older men mediated by frontal lateralization.' *Neuroimage* (2015). DOI:10.1016/j.neuroimage.2015.09.062.

Rovio, S. et al. 'Leisure-time physical activity at midlife and the risk of dementia and Alzheimer's disease.' *Lancet Neurology* (2005).

Sanchez, M. et al. 'BDNF polymorphism predicts the rate of decline in skilled task performance and hippocampal volume in healthy individuals.' *Translational Psychiatry* (2011). DOI:10.1038/tp.2011.47.

Tan, Q. et al. 'Midlife and late-life cardiorespiratory fitness and brain volume changes in late adulthood: results from the Baltimore longitudinal study of aging.' *The Journals of Gerontology: Series A, Biological Sciences and Medical Sciences* (2016). DOI:10.1093/gerona/glv041.

Wueve, J. et al. 'Physical activity, including walking, and cognitive function in older women.' *JAMA* 292; 12 (2004): 1454–61.

9. A Stone Age Brain in the Digital Age

Florio, M. et al. 'Human-specific ARHGAPIIB promotes basal progenitor amplification and neocortex expansion.' *Science* (2015). DOI:10.1126/scienceaaa1975.

Raichlen, D. et al. 'Linking brains and brawn: exercise and the evolution of human neurobiology.' *Proceedings of the Royal Society B: Biological Sciences* (2013). DOI:10.1098/rspb.2012.2250.

Raichlen, D. et al. 'Relation between exercise capacity and brain size in mammals.' *PLoS One* 6; 6 (2011): e20601.

ACKNOWLEDGEMENTS

FIRST, AN ENORMOUS *thank you* to my brother Björn Hansen, who gave me priceless input and suggested several ideas I would never have thought of on my own. Also, a big *thank you* to my mother Vanja Hansen for all her encouragement and support.

I'd like to thank – in no specific order – the following people, who have each in their own way contributed good ideas, inspiration and feedback during this journey: Karl Tobiesen, Simon Kyaga, Martin Lorentzon, Jonas Pettersson, Carl Johan Sundberg, Minna Tunberger, Mats Thorén, Otto Ankarcrona, Mattias Olsson, Daniel Ek, Jakob Endler, Tahir Jamil, Johannes Croner, Kristoffer Ahlbom, Gustaf Vahlne, Anders Berntsson, Erik Telander and Lars Frick. It has been a true privilege tossing ideas back and forth with you all.

I want to offer a special *thank you* to Cecilia Viklund and Kerstin Bergfors at Bonnier Fakta, and to my editor Anna Paljak. Thanks to Frederico Ambrosini at Salomonson Agency for bringing my books to the world, and Jessica Anderson, Evangeline Stanford and the whole team at Vermilion for doing such a great job publishing my books in the UK.

INDEX

Newton, Isaac 154–5
NGF *see* nerve growth factor
nicotine 99
Nietzsche, Friedrich 159
noise levels, internal 71–2, 73, 85
nomadic peoples 80–2, 196
noradrenaline
  and concentration 87
  and depression 97, 98–9, 106
  functions 99
nucleus accumbens (reward centre)
    64–7, 85
nutrition 141, 189, 192, 193
  see also food
nutritional supplements 205

obesity 74, 103–4, 200
occipital lobe 3–4, 7
oestrogen, and depression 103–4
Okinawa 189
opium 109–10
Oppezzo, Marily 151
optic nerve 7
Organisation for Economic
    Cooperation and Development
    (OECD) 163
overweight
  and academic achievement
    165, 168–9
  and depression 103–4
  see also obesity
oxazepam 32–3
oxygen supply 16, 25, 31

pain, memory of 134–5
pain relief 109–11, 114–15
panic attacks 20, 23, 29, 45, 48, 51–6
  prevention 54–5, 56
parietal lobe 7, 61
pattern separation 139–40
pedometers 168, 197
Peek, Kim 14–16
perseverance 154–5
personality, positive 108–9
PET *see* positron emission tomography
physical education 164

physical exercise 2–5, 209–10
  and ageing 179–90
  and attention deficit hyperactivity
    disorder 68, 76–9, 84
  and children 163–78
  and concentration 59–87
  and creativity 147–62
  and depression 89–117
  as drug 109
  duration 87, 146, 162, 178
  feelgood factor 65, 109
  frequency 87, 146, 162, 178
  and gamma-aminobutyric acid 34
  high-intensity 26, 125–6, 130–1,
    152, 172, 183
  intensity of 172, 178
  and learning 125–30
  making it a habit 56
  and memory 119–46
  in the morning 87
  move away from 196–203
  and neurogenesis 106
  and panic attacks 54–5
  and personality traits 108–9
  and the positive–negative axis 10
  and stress 18, 19–57
  and survival 36
  see also specific type of physical exercise
physical fitness
  and academic achievement
    165–7, 175–6
  and ageing 180
  and brain size 165–6
  and children 165–7
  and concentration 60–1, 174–6
  and creativity 153
  and Intelligence Quotient 174–5
  lifetime benefits of 175–6
  and memory 119, 122, 124
  and stress 25–7
physical inactivity 84–5
  trend towards 196–203
  see also sedentary lifestyle
piano playing 126–30
pig studies 110
pilots 182–3

ABOUT THE AUTHOR

Dr Anders Hansen is a Swedish psychiatrist, speaker and international bestselling author with his own TV series exploring the human brain. Dr Hansen's books have sold millions of copies globally and topped bestseller lists around the world. He is the winner of the book of the year Big Health Award 2017 and 2019, and Sweden's Mensa Prize 2018.

Dr Hansen is also the author of *The Happiness Cure*, *The Attention Fix* and *The ADHD Advantage*.

Also by Dr Anders Hansen

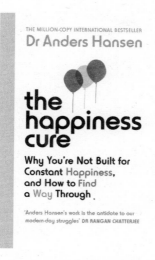

The Happiness Cure

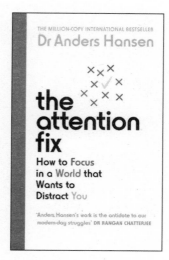

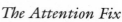

The Attention Fix

The ADHD Advantage